Baked!

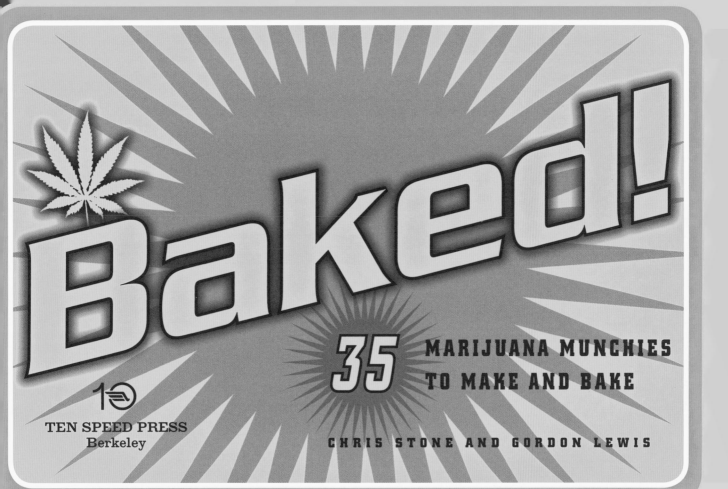

Baked!

35 MARIJUANA MUNCHIES TO MAKE AND BAKE

TEN SPEED PRESS
Berkeley

CHRIS STONE AND GORDON LEWIS

Copyright © 2010 by
Elephant Book Company Limited

Illustrations copyright © 2010 by
Elephant Book Company Limited

Published in the United States by Ten Speed Press, an
imprint of the Crown Publishing Group, a division of
Random House, Inc., New York, by arrangement with Elephant
Book Company Limited, 35 Fournier Street,
London E1 6QE, United Kingdom

www.crownpublishing.com
www.tenspeed.com

Ten Speed Press and the Ten Speed colophon are registered
trademarks of Random House, Inc.

Editorial Director: Will Steeds
Project Editor: Laura Ward
Cover and Interior Design: Lindsey Johns
Illustrator: Robert Brandt
Copy Editor: Karen Stein
Production: Robert Paulley
Color Reproduction:
Modern Age Repro House Ltd., Hong Kong

Ten Speed Press Editor: Julie Bennett

Library of Congress Cataloging-in-Publication Data

Stone, Chris, 1973–
  Baked! : 35 marijuana munchies to make and bake / Chris Stone
and Gordon Lewis.
     p. cm.
  Summary: "A cookbook for cannabis lovers, featuring 35 recipes
for sweet and savory treats made with marijuana"—Provided by
publisher.
  1. Cooking (Marijuana) 2. Desserts. I. Lewis, Gordon, 1947– II.
Title.
  TX819.M25S86 2010
  641.6'379—dc22

                                2010022423

ISBN 978-1-58008-477-2

Printed in China

10 9 8 7 6 5 4 3 2

Second Edition

Contents

Introduction

In our modern world, smoking (both grass and tobacco) is increasingly becoming socially unacceptable. Bars and restaurants in many countries worldwide have banned the legal variety, and, heaven forbid, there are even plans afoot to curb the coffee shop culture of Amsterdam, Europe's pothead mecca. And that doesn't even include health lobbyists' efforts. So, deprived of his or her traditional joint, what's a poor stoner to do?

The truth is that many lovers of the wacky tobaccy are donning their aprons and cooking with cannabis instead. And you should, too. Although there have been several books published on cannabis cooking over the years (there was even a recipe for hashish fudge in the Alice B. Toklas Cookbook way back in 1947!), this is the first book to focus solely on baking. You will find in these pages thirty-five recipes for the sweetest of snacks and the yummiest of savories, from Mind Blowin' Scones and Fruity Loopy Loaf to Ganja Garlic Heads and Herbal Quiche. None of the recipes take more than an hour to make, although some may be in the oven for up to an hour and others occasionally involve a couple of hours' chill time—but nothing new to you there. And the instructions are so simple even a stoner can follow them.

So, following a quick history lesson (see opposite), let's head for the kitchen to get baking and get baked! Just remember to turn the oven off when you've finished.

A History of Cannabis Cooking

Cooking with cannabis may seem like a radical departure from the traditional j, but in fact people were ingesting cannabis long before anyone sparked up a primitive reefer. Records state that Chinese emperor Shen Nung (2737 BCE) used cannabis as an oral medicine.

There are many other examples through history. In India, the mystical Shiva, known as "Lord of the Bhang," was the first eater of cannabis leaves; modern-day Sadhus still chew leaves in his honor. The Indian subcontinent has also given us the potent drink, Bhang, a heady mix of cannabis, milk, yogurt, almonds, and spices. In ancient Greece, the philosopher Democritus (460–360 BCE) recorded that cannabis was drunk with wine and myrrh to aid visions, while rich Romans in the second century CE were partial to a cannabis-seed dessert. In the eleventh century, Arabs developed sweets made from cannabis—known as mahjoun—while two hundred years later the religious sect of Sufis from the Middle East chewed a cannabis-laden gum to get in touch with God.

Then, in 1884, the world's first coffee shop opened in Paris. The Club des Hashichins was dedicated to exploring drug-induced experiences and counted among its members the likes of Charles Baudelaire and Alexandre Dumas. The club's cofounder, Dr Jacques-Joseph, would often administer to members a "green paste" of hash, mixed with a strong Arabic coffee. Nice.

All the recipes in this book are rated from one to five in the following categories:

HOW HIGH?:
The potency of the recipe—the greater the number of leaves shown, the more stoned you will get.

DIFFICULTY:
Indicates the complexity of the recipe for a home chef such as yourself.

MAKIN' TIME:
How long (in minutes) the recipe takes to prepare, from start to oven.

BAKIN' TIME:
How long (in minutes) the bread, cookie, pastry, or savory dish takes to cook.

THE BASICS OF GETTING BAKED

chapter 1

"Everyone should eat hashish . . . but only once."

Salvador Dalí

Dali might have been a decent painter but he clearly knew little about cannabis. As long as you pay attention to the whys and wherefores of cannabis cooking explained in this chapter (the advantages of baking with marijuana, preparation of your weed, and dosage), you will enjoy a long and fruitful relationship with ganja gastronomy. Enjoy.

Why Eat Your Weed?

RAW DEAL
Don't eat raw cannabis. It tastes awful and produces a slow-acting and unpredictable high.

So, what's better, smoking a fat j or eating a cannabis cookie? Of course, in a social setting there's nothing like a good smoke, but, this aside, when you assess the pros and cons of smoking weed versus eating it, cannabis cooking wins out every time.

Here are the factors:

Discretion—Burned cannabis is pungent and, though you might love the smell, there are many other noses that disapprove (especially those of the feds). Smoking a joint is far from discreet, whereas eating an innocent hash cake will arouse no suspicion whatsoever—until you start giggling uncontrollably and falling over, that is.

Health factor—Cannabis itself is not carcinogenic but it often contains impurities (depending on its provenance) that, when burned and inhaled, can cause major health issues. And if you roll your weed with tobacco, you're taking some obvious risks. Eating properly cooked ganja is free of health risks. In fact, cannabis is a nutritious fiber, its seed a source of edible oil. So there.

The high—The active ingredient in your weed (the part that gets you wasted) is called cannibinoids. The most pertinent of these is delta 9-tetrahydracannabinol ("THC" to you and me). THC is more effective if dissolved in fats—they link onto the THC molecules and make absorption far more effective. If prepared and cooked correctly, the cannabis will give you a high that is more intense, cerebral, and longer lasting than the buzz you will get from a couple of bong hits. Many ganja gourmets have likened the buzz to an LSD trip, so be careful with your dosage levels (see page 17).

Economy–It's obvious, but when you smoke a joint, most of the good stuff drifts off into the atmosphere in between tokes, and doesn't get into your lungs (and bloodstream), where it would take effect. Similarly, smoking is wasteful in that, with grass, only the buds are smoked. The leaves, stalks, and seeds are thrown away. But with cooking you can use every part of the plant. The process of cooking Boosted Butter (see page 12) breaks down these undesirable parts of the plant and assimilates whatever active compounds are present.

Pain relief–Cooked cannabis is an especially popular means of pain relief for people suffering from chronic illnesses like multiple sclerosis and arthritis. And the high lasts longer.

Waiting for the hit

One key difference between smoking weed and ingesting it, though it is certainly not a negative, does deserve special attention–timing. When you inhale smoke, the THC reaches your bloodstream quickly; the hit is more or less instantaneous and the high may last an hour. Eating cannabis is very different. The chronic needs to be digested (via your gut) along with the rest of your food and will take time to reach your bloodstream–as much as two hours–and the effects may last for as long as eight hours.

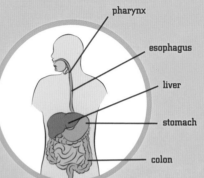

pharynx

esophagus

liver

stomach

colon

Basically, err on the side of caution, and if you're planning on a large culinary cannabis session, take the rest of the day off.

LESS IS MORE

Eat your marijuana morsels as small pieces of snack food. Big dishes take longer to digest and get into the bloodstream. You don't want to invite your buddies over for a dope dinner and wind up being high as a kite at three in the morning, long after everyone's gone home.

Preparing Your Pot

There are three main ways to incorporate your stash into the recipes that follow—butter, oil, and ground raw cannabis. Each method requires preparation before you start making the recipes. Here's a guide to what to do.

How to Make Boosted Butter

Boosted Butter is the best way to assimilate the goodness from your chronic into any recipe. It can be stored for months without spoiling.

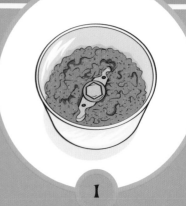

I

I Grind your stash into a very fine powder.

You will need:

2 cups (455 g) butter

2 ounces (55 g) high-quality bud, hash, or leaf

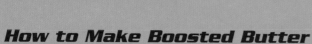

MEASUREMENTS

Two ounces might sound like a lot of weed to lay your hands on. And the cost of acquiring it may be prohibitive. However, most growers will happily give you a few bags of cannabis leaves (they are next to useless for smoking purposes) for free. If that's not an option, just scale down your pot-to-butter ratio accordingly—for example, 1/2 cup (1/4 pound/113 g) of butter and 1/2 ounce (14 g) of weed.

DREAMY DRINK

Leftover leafy material from the process of making Boosted Butter can be simmered in hot milk or vodka to make a tasty and potent drink.

2 In a large, heavy saucepan, bring about 3 cups (720 ml) water to a boil.

3

2

3 Add the butter and ground cannabis to the boiling water. When the butter has melted, reduce the heat, cover the pan, and simmer for approximately 2 hours, stirring occasionally. Turn off the heat and let the solution rest for 2 to 3 minutes.

4 Strain your cannabis-rich liquid through a sieve or cheesecloth into a separate container to remove any unwanted particles. Any debris that remains can be discarded or consumed separately (see box).

4

5 Let the butter liquid cool completely, then cover the bowl and place in a refrigerator overnight to separate.

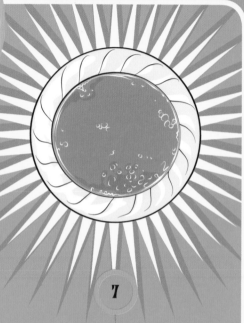

6 In the morning you will note that a deep layer of hardened butter has formed at the top of the bowl. Discard the water that remains. (Don't drink it, you fool!)

WHAT TO USE

While the "budding" cannabis chef can use any part of the marijuana plant for cooking, hashish (as long as it's of high quality) is the best choice, because much of the preparation has already taken place during its manufacture (in which bud is repeatedly strained and compressed to turn it into hash) and it dissolves well in fat.

7 Keep the butter refrigerated (or ideally frozen) to ensure it does not go bad. You now have a supply of butter that can be substituted for normal fat in any recipe. You can even spread it on toast!

How to Make Augmented Olive Oil

The advantage of Augmented Olive Oil is that you can store it for a long time at ordinary room temperature without it going bad.

You will need:

---

2 cups [480 ml] olive oil

---

2 ounces [55 g] grass or hash

I In a large, heavy saucepan, heat the oil over medium heat until hot but not boiling (it must not boil at any time). Lower the heat to keep it at a steady temperature.

OIL HINTS

You can store the oil in its original bottle if you like, but keep it in a cupboard out of the light, which can lower its potency. When you want to use it, don't forget to give it a good shake first.

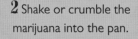

2 Shake or crumble the marijuana into the pan.

3 Maintain that steady temperature for 2 hours. Keep an eye on it for the first half hour or so, stirring every ten minutes. If at any time it should start to boil, just lift the pan off the heat and let it cool down a bit; then turn the heat down slightly. Do this a couple of times and you should find the right heat. After a while the oil might turn a little bit green or brown due to the resin extraction.

4 After 2 hours, remove the pan from the heat and let cool for about a half hour. Then strain the liquid a couple of times, and you're there.

How to Make Pot Powder

Pot Powder is simply a grand term for ground cannabis. You can use bud, hash, or leaf, although the potency will vary. If using leaf or bud, ensure that it's dry and crisp enough to be crumbled between your fingers. A minute in an oven or microwave will do the trick.

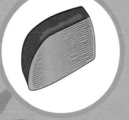

Bud

Hash

I First remove the stalks and any unwanted debris and place the leaves in a food processor.

2 Process until it has a flour-like consistency.

3 Using a knife, work the Pot Powder though a sieve to break down any stubborn pieces. The fine dust that is generated during this process is precious stuff, high in THC, so be careful not to let it escape.

4 Empty the sieved Pot Powder into an airtight container and keep refrigerated.

HASH FLOUR

Hash crumbles naturally when exposed to light heat, as you will know from joint rolling. A fine grater or mortar and pestle can also be used for grinding. For sticky, oily resin, just use a sharp knife to cut the hash into very small pieces—it will fully dissolve when cooked.

Get Dosed!

	MILD	NORMAL	EXTREME
Boosted Butter	1/2 tsp. (2.5 g)	1 tsp. (5 g)	1.5 tsp. (7.5 g)
Augmented Olive Oil	1/2 tsp. (2.5 g)	1 tsp. (5 g)	1.5 tsp. (7.5 g)
Pot Powder	1/4 tsp. (.62 g)	1/2 tsp. (1.25 g)	3/4 tsp. (1.875 g)

As previously noted, the greatest mistake you can make with ganja gastronomy is with the dosage.

No one's expecting you to produce four-star cuisine, and if your finished dish looks like dog food, nobody will care as long as everyone gets pleasantly wasted. But mess up the special ingredient and there'll be trouble.

Too little and you end up waiting for a hit that never arrives; too much, and you could be scraping dinner guests off the ceiling for days afterward. As a rule of thumb, a single dose would be about half a teaspoon of ground weed or hash.

Pay attention to the information in the charts above and load your recipes accordingly. However, please note that these figures are only a basic guide. The degree to which any individual is affected is the result of many variables—the ingredients used; the way the food has been prepared; the quality of the dope; and the person's weight, metabolism, state of mind, and experience of cannabis use.

Because these values are approximate, please experiment with dosage levels for people of different weights and experience. All recipes are calculated on the basis of a "normal" dosage.

SMOKE TEST

If you're unsure about the potency of a particular strain of weed, don't just put it in the recipe and hope for the best. Smoke a small sample. If you get a huge buzz off a few tokes, then you know the effect will be similarly huge when baked and can distribute accordingly.

MEASUREMENTS

Measurements are in level teaspoons and are based on the dosage for an experienced male stoner of average weight—for example, 160 pounds (72 kg).

The Kitchen

The kitchen may be unfamiliar territory for you. Sure, you've visited it frequently in the past to grab munchies from the fridge but in order to bake stuff in there, you're gonna have to get properly acquainted.

You don't need lots of equipment to bake most of the dishes in this book. Here are the things you will need:

- One or two baking pans of different sizes

- A couple of flat baking sheets, preferably with a lip along one long side

- One or two muffin pans

- A whisk

- A couple of wooden spoons

- A sieve

- A rolling pin (a straight-sided bottle can make a good stand-in)

- Mixing bowls

DON'T INCINERATE IT

While heating cannabis through the cooking process is proven to release more cannabinoids, overcooking (or exposing to extreme heat) will destroy much of the THC. So pay close attention to the cooking temperatures in the recipes.

OUTTA SIGHT

Boosted Butter, Augmented Olive Oil, and all the finished recipes in this book look (and largely taste) like regular food, so ensure that all cannabinated food is kept well out of the reach of minors, or indeed, of anyone who won't take kindly to a large dose of the magic herb.

If you're strapped for cash, look for the cheap disposable metal foil baking pans and sheets at your grocery store—it's amazing how many times you can use them before they wear out. Or, hit the garage sales.

Now, my little canna-chefs, you're ready to start cooking up some treats. Soon you'll be producing top-notch food like these tasty muffins. Good luck.

A NOTE ON THE RECIPES

The recipes that follow utilize a quantity of pre-prepared Boosted Butter (which is sometimes supplemented with normal butter) and Augmented Olive Oil. The quantity of chronic used in the butter and oil in each recipe is based on the dosage table on page 17. If you do not have any Boosted Butter and wish to use untreated ground cannabis instead, please refer to the dosage table. Powdered cannabis, when required, should be added with the dry ingredients in each recipe.

Dosage levels for Boosted Butter and Augmented Olive Oil are measured in teaspoons, and then multiplied by the number of cakes, bread servings, biscuits, and the like produced by the recipe—for example, in Mind Blowin' Scones, 1 teaspoon (5g) x 12 scones = 60g. Easy, isn't it?

BLOWIN' BISCUITS AND COOKIES

"Space cake cookies I discover who I am
I'm a dusted old bummy Hurdy Gurdy Man."

"Car Thief" by the Beastie Boys

Cookies are often the only things some people have ever baked—usually as a kid at their mother's side. There's a good reason for this, as they are incredibly simple to make. So simple, in fact, that even a dumbass stoner like you is capable of producing great results. So tie on that flowery apron and get to it.

Boom-Boom Biscuits

Packs a punch

These biscuits are a baker's favorite. They're made with relatively few ingredients, including, of course, a generous helping of Boosted Butter. It's ironic that the culinary skill required here is to get the biscuits to rise, while you will be positively slumped after eating one. A tasty topping of Jive Jam will help you on your way.

How High?:
🌿 🌿 🌿 🌿 🌿

Difficulty:
🌿 🌿 🌿 🌿

Makin' Time:
30 minutes

Bakin' Time:
10–12 minutes

2 cups (300 g) all-purpose flour, plus additional for rolling

¼ teaspoon baking soda

1 tablespoon baking powder

1 teaspoon kosher salt or sea salt

3 tablespoons plus 2 teaspoons (50 g) Boosted Butter (page 12), chilled and cut into cubes

2 ½ tablespoons (35 g) butter, chilled and cut into cubes

Approximately ¾ cup (165 ml) buttermilk

Makes about 10 biscuits

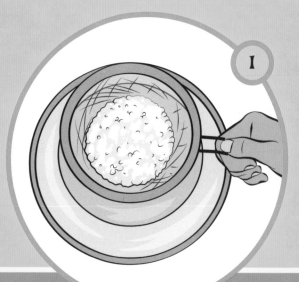

I Preheat the oven to 450°F (230°C/gas mark 8). Sift the flour, baking soda, baking powder, and salt into a large mixing bowl.

2 Using a pastry blender or a kitchen knife, cut the butters into the flour mixture until it resembles coarse crumbs.

3 Stir in just enough buttermilk to combine everything into a softish dough.

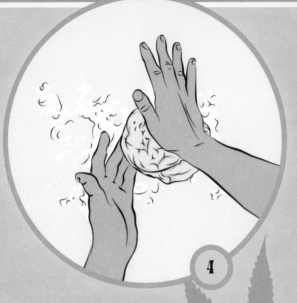

4 Turn the dough out on to a floured board. Gently pat it until the dough is about ½ inch (1.25 cm) thick.

5 Use a 2⅜-inch (6-cm) cutter to cut out about 10 rounds, re-rolling the trimmings as necessary.

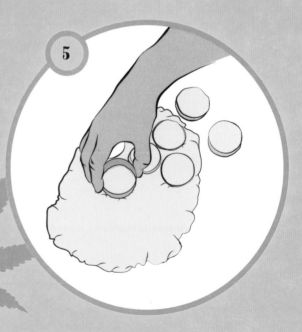

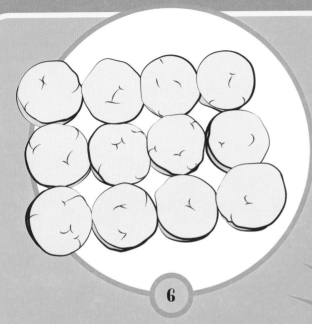

6

7 Bake for 10 to 12 minutes, until the tops are a beautiful light brown. Serve with some Jive Jam (page 127), and settle back and wait for the rush.

7

6 Place the biscuits on a lightly greased cookie sheet. If you would like them to be tall and have soft sides, place them so they are touching each other as shown; if you would prefer them "crusty" and less risen, place them about 1 inch (2.5 cm) apart.

Caribbean Cookies

Tropical delight

Ah, the Caribbean, every vacationer's dream—palm trees, soft sand, warm oceans, fat Jamaican spliffs, and now sweet-tasting, dope-laced cookies. If the great Bob Marley had ever stopped skinning up long enough to venture into his kitchen, he'd probably have made these, too. They're perfect with an afternoon piña colada.

I

How High?:
🌿 🌿 🌿

Difficulty:
🌿 🌿 🌿

Makin' Time:
20 minutes, plus
2 hours chillin'

Bakin' Time:
10–12 minutes

²/₃ cup (150 g) Boosted Butter (page 12), softened

2 tablespoons (25 g) butter, softened

½ cup (100 g) granulated sugar

½ cup (100 g) brown sugar, lightly packed

½ teaspoon baking soda

¼ teaspoon salt

2 eggs

1 teaspoon vanilla extract

2 cups (300 g) all-purpose flour

⅓ cup (30 g) shredded sweetened coconut

1 tablespoon grated lime zest

3 tablespoons lime juice (from about 1 lime)

¼ cup (30 g) confectioners' sugar

Makes about 30 cookies

I In the bowl of a stand mixer, or in a large bowl with a hand-held electric mixer, place the butters, the granulated and brown sugars ("Brown sugar, how come you taste so good?"), baking soda, and salt, and beat at moderate speed for about 3 minutes to blend well.

2 Beat in the eggs and vanilla extract. Reduce the mixer speed and add the flour gradually. Finally, stir in the coconut, lime zest, and lime juice until well incorporated.

3 On a lightly floured surface, roll the dough into a 10-inch (25 cm) log and wrap tightly with plastic wrap. Chill the dough for 2 hours in the refrigerator, until firm.

BOOZE BOOST
A little dash of dark rum added with the vanilla will make these cookies even more evocative of island life and, crucially, guarantee that you will become even more wasted.

4 When ready to bake, preheat the oven to 375°F (190°C/gas mark 5). Cut the chilled cookie dough log crosswise into rounds about 1/3 inch (.75 cm) thick.

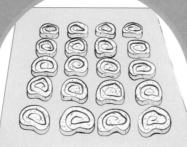

5

6 Leave to cool on the sheet for a minute; then transfer to a wire rack to cool completely. Using a sifter, sprinkle the tops of the cookies with confectioners' sugar (or your finest weed) while still warm.

6

4

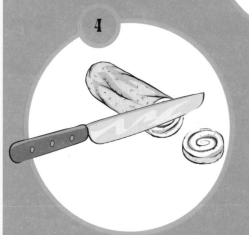

5 Place the cookies on an ungreased baking sheet a couple of inches apart and bake for 10 to 12 minutes, until the edges are a light golden brown.

Alice B. Toklas's Cookies

The original and the best

The life partner of writer Gertrude Stein, Toklas was something of a peripheral figure until she famously included a recipe for "Haschich Fudge" (more like brownies, in fact) in her 1954 memoir "The Alice B. Toklas Cookbook." Thereafter, her name became synonymous with cannabis foods. This cookie recipe, loosely based on her original, certainly does justice to her memory. Eat with pride.

How High?:

Difficulty:

Makin' Time:
15 minutes

Bakin' Time:
15 minutes

I Preheat the oven to 325°F (160°C/gas mark 3). In a medium-sized mixing bowl, stir together the flour, cinnamon, baking soda, and salt.

2 cups (300 g) all-purpose flour

1/2 teaspoon ground cinnamon

1 teaspoon baking soda

1/2 teaspoon salt

6 tablespoons (90 g) Boosted Butter (page 12). at room temperature

1/2 cup plus 2 tablespoons (135 g) butter. at room temperature

3/4 cup (150 g) firmly packed golden brown sugar

1 1/2 teaspoons vanilla extract

1/2 teaspoon almond extract

2 large eggs

2 cups (250 g) coarsely chopped pecans

2 cups (360 g) semisweet chocolate chips

Makes about 18 cookies

29

2 In a large bowl, using a balloon whisk or an electric mixer at low speed, beat (meaning "stir vigorously," not "attack with a baseball bat") the butters, brown sugar, vanilla extract, and almond extract until well blended.

2

3

3 Add the eggs and beat until the mixture is fluffy. Then beat in the flour mixture a large spoonful at a time.

4 Stir the pecans and chocolate chips into the dough.

4

5 Drop rounded tablespoonfuls in well-spaced mounds on ungreased baking sheets. Flatten each slightly with the back of a spoon.

6 Bake the cookies until their edges begin to brown but the centers are still soft, about 15 minutes. Let cool on the baking sheets for 2 minutes; then transfer to wire racks to cool completely.

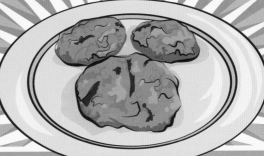

TOKIN'
Many stoners believe that this slang term for inhaling cannabis smoke comes from Toklas.

Mind-Blowin' Scones

Upper-class munchies

The perfect accompaniment to a cup of tea, these scones are really easy to bake and can be eaten on their own or with a little jive jam and cream. The only possible drawback to this recipe is the inclusion of dried fruit, which is not renowned as munchie food. So if any of your buddies is gripped by "chronic" fear and complains about the prevalence of mouse droppings, reassure your friend that these are in fact raisins.

How High?:
✳ ✳ ✳ ✳ ✳

Difficulty:
✳ ✳ ✳ ✳ ✳

Makin' Time:
20 minutes

Bakin' Time:
15 minutes

2 ½ cups (375 g) all-purpose flour, plus additional for rolling

3 ½ teaspoons baking powder

½ teaspoon salt

3 tablespoons super-fine sugar

¼ cup (60 g) Boosted Butter (page 12), chilled, cut into cubes

1 tablespoon butter, chilled, cut into cubes

1 cup (170 g) seedless raisins, soaked in hot water and drained

2 eggs, lightly beaten

½ cup (125 ml) heavy cream

1 tablespoon vanilla extract

Makes about 12 scones

I Preheat the oven to 400°F (200°C/ gas mark 6) and lightly butter a baking sheet. Sift the flour, baking powder, and salt into a mixing bowl; then add the sugar and the butters.

2 Cut in the butter until the mixture resembles coarse crumbs; then stir in raisins, eggs, cream, and vanilla extract, and mix until a dough forms.

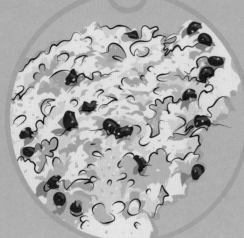

3 Turn out the dough onto a floured board and knead (see box on page 34) it briefly. Roll out to a thickness of about 1 inch (2.5 cm).

BURNIN' DOWN THE HOUSE

Many of the recipes in this book begin with the instruction to preheat the oven. But do, of course, turn off the oven once you're through cooking. It's not a cost-efficient way to heat your house and could lead to a serious fire.

4 Cut out rounds with 2-inch (5 cm) diameter using a biscuit cutter, glass, or cup.

5 Place the rounds well spaced on the baking sheet and bake for about 15 minutes, or until the tops of the scones are brown. Let stand for a minute on a wire rack. Serve warm.

COOKING PRACTICE

Kneading is the process of working a dough by folding it and pushing it with the heels of the hands, turning it over and over to help it develop a smooth, elastic texture. This is, like, a proper skill, so you will need to practice it (while sober) in order to avoid getting a lumpy mess. Note the distinction in spelling and meaning here. You need a smoke, but you knead bread.

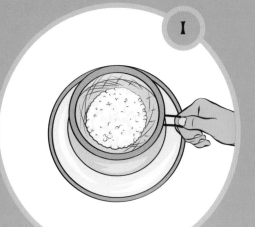

Munchie People

Off with their heads . . . and limbs

As a dedicated smoker, and now cannabis chef of growing repute, you're far too irresponsible to have real children of your own. But that doesn't preclude you from making your own pretend little people in the kitchen, using many of the techniques you've already learned. But don't grow too attached to your cookie offspring (you weirdo), as it is your duty to eat them, perhaps with a cup of tea and a fat j.

How High?:
🌿 🌿 🌿 🌿

Difficulty:
🌿 🌿 🌿

Makin' Time:
30 minutes, plus
2 hours chillin'

Bakin' Time:
9–14 minutes

I In a medium bowl, sift or whisk together the flour, salt, baking soda, spices, and Pot Powder. Set aside.

3 cups (450 g) all-purpose flour, plus additional for rolling

1/4 teaspoon salt

3/4 teaspoon baking soda

2 teaspoons ground ginger

1 teaspoon ground cinnamon

1/4 teaspoon freshly grated nutmeg

6 1/2 teaspoons Pot Powder (page 16)

1/2 cup (115 g) Boosted Butter (page 12), at room temperature

1/2 cup (115 g) granulated sugar

1 large egg

2/3 cup (150 ml) light molasses

Makes about 36 cookies

2 In the bowl of a stand mixer fitted with the paddle attachment, or in a large bowl with a hand-held electric mixer, cream together the Boosted Butter and sugar until light and fluffy. Add the egg and molasses, and beat until well combined. Gradually add the flour mixture, beating until incorporated.

4 When ready to bake, preheat the oven to 350°F (180°C/gas mark 4) and place a rack in the center of the oven. Line 2 baking sheets with parchment paper and set aside while you roll out the dough.

3

4

2

3 Divide the dough in half, wrap each half in plastic wrap, and refrigerate for at least 2 hours or overnight.

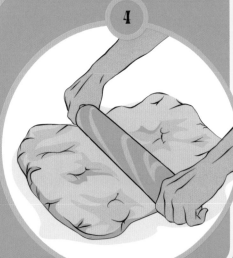

BAKED!

5 On a lightly floured surface, roll out the dough to a thickness of about 1/4 inch (.5 cm). Using a gingerbread-person cutter, cut out the cookies. With a spatula, lift the cookies and place them on the baking sheet about 1 inch (2.5 cm) apart.

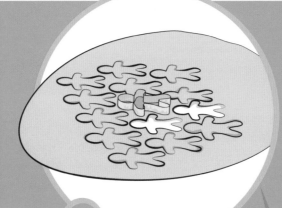

5

6 Bake the cookies for 9 to 14 minutes, depending on their size, until firm and edges are just beginning to brown. Remove from the oven and let cool on the baking sheet for about 1 minute. When cookies are firm enough to move, transfer to a wire rack to cool completely.

6

FINISHING TOUCHES

While the cookies are still warm, you can press chopped dried fruit or candies into the dough for eyes and buttons to make them look even more like little people. For a final flourish, add little reefers to the mouths of your cookie men. So that's, like, a man made of weed, who's smoking weed, and you're gonna eat him. Whoa, that's a head trip, man.

Spaced Shortbread

Scottish grub

Historically a product of Scotland, the shortbread style of cookie is known for its crumbly texture, the cause of which is the cookie's high fat content. So, not only will you drop crumbs down your front while eating it but you will also put on weight. Still, the weed content in this shortbread will ensure that any such concerns are far from your mind.

How High?:
🍁 🍁 🍁

Difficulty:
🍁 🍁 🍁

Makin' Time:
20 minutes, plus 1¼ hours chillin'

Bakin' Time:
15–20 minutes

7 tablespoons (100 g) Boosted Butter (page 12), at room temperature
1 tablespoon (115 g) butter, at room temperature
½ cup (115 g) super-fine sugar, plus additional for sprinkling
1 teaspoon vanilla extract
2 cups (300 g) all-purpose flour
¼ teaspoon salt

Makes about 20 cookies

I In the bowl of an electric mixer (or in a medium bowl with a wooden spoon or hand-held electric mixer), cream the butters until smooth, about 1 minute. Add the sugar and beat until even in texture, about 2 minutes. Beat in the vanilla extract.

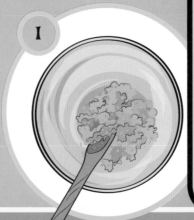

I

VARIATIONS

You can vary the flavor of these delicious cookies by adding chocolate chips, chopped orange or lemon zest, for example. You can also make delicious spiced shortbread by using brown sugar in place of the super-fine sugar and adding ½ teaspoon of ground spice, such as cinnamon or cardamon. Remember that the shortbread dough needs an hour's chilling, followed by another 15 minutes once cut into shapes.

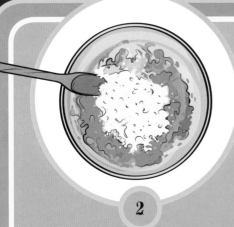

2

3 On a lightly floured surface, roll out the dough to 1/4 inch (.5 cm) thick. Cut into rounds, or whatever shapes you wish, using a lightly floured cookie cutter. Place the cookies on the prepared baking sheets, prick lightly with a fork, and chill for about 15 minutes. This will firm up the dough so the cookies keep their shape when baked.

2 Sift the flour into a small bowl and stir in the salt. Then gently stir the flour mixture into the butter-and-sugar mixture until just incorporated. Flatten the dough into a disk shape, wrap in plastic wrap, and chill for at least an hour. You can sit down and smoke a reefer while you wait. Preheat the oven to 350°F (180°C/gas mark 4) and line 2 baking sheets with parchment paper.

3

4

4 Sprinkle the top of each cookie with a little sugar and bake for 15 to 20 minutes, until the cookies are lightly browned. Let cool on baking sheets on wire racks.

chapter 3

CHILLIN' CAKES, BREADS, AND MUFFINS

"All sorrows are bearable, if there is bread."

Miguel de Cervantes

Unlike ordinary bread, which requires lots of energetic kneading and lengthy periods of resting, most of the sweet breads in this chapter simply involve mixing all the ingredients and putting them straight into the oven. In fact, about the only way you can get less-than-perfect results with most of these recipes is to overbeat the mixture.

Wake-and-Bake Breakfast Rolls

Morning glory

As a committed stoner, you're probably unused to eating at a conventional breakfast time—instead, you're either sleeping off the effects of last night's bongs, or, worse, just heading off to bed. However, these breakfast rolls are well worth getting up for, and the special ingredient will put a spring in your step. Just don't eat all twenty.

How High?:
✳ ✳ ✳ ✳ ✳

Difficulty:
✳ ✳ ✳ ✳ ✳

Makin' Time:
30 minutes, plus 2–2½ hours chillin' and rising

Bakin' Time:
15–20 minutes

---

1 package (¼ ounce/ 7 g) active dry yeast

1 ½ cups (350 ml) warm milk

7 tablespoons (100 g) Boosted Butter (page 12), melted

2 eggs, lightly beaten

3 tablespoons sugar (or more to taste)

2 teaspoons sea salt

1 ½ teaspoons Pot Powder (page 16)

3 ½ cups (525 g) bread flour or all-purpose flour, plus additional for kneading

Melted butter, for brushing the tops of the rolls

Makes 20 rolls

I In a large mixing bowl, add the yeast to the warm milk and let dissolve. Add the Boosted Butter, eggs, sugar, salt, and Pot Powder and stir.

2 Gradually incorporate the flour about 1/2 cup at a time and stir until the dough is smooth and starts to come away from the side of the bowl. (If this starts to happen before all the flour is added, don't add the remaining flour.)

3 Turn out the dough on a lightly floured surface and knead until it feels smooth, soft, and springy. If it gets sticky at any time, don't panic, man. Just sprinkle it with more flour and knead that in.

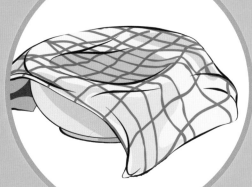

4 Put the dough in a buttered bowl, cover with a damp cloth, and leave in a warm, draft-free place to rise for 45 minutes to 1 hour, until doubled in size. Treat yourself to a smoke and a nap while you wait.

5 Punch the dough down thoroughly, then put it back in the bowl, cover, and let rise again for about an hour until about doubled in size. Punch the dough down again and divide it into 16 to 20 equal pieces (you can weigh them to make sure they are equal in size, if you like).

6

7 Cover loosely with foil, plastic wrap, or a clean kitchen towel, and leave to rise in a warm place until doubled in size again, about 45 minutes.

5

6 Roll each into a ball on the palm of one hand, rotating the dough with the other hand until smooth and round. (A bit of finesse is required here— maybe you shouldn't have had that smoke.) Place snugly together on a baking sheet to encourage them to rise.

8 Put a bowl of hot water in the oven (to make a steamy atmosphere in the oven that will help the rolls rise) and preheat the oven to 450°F (210°C/gas mark 6). Bake the rolls for 15 to 20 minutes until the crusts are light brown all over. Remove from the oven and immediately brush lightly with melted butter.

9 Allow to cool slightly and serve warm.

QUICK START
You need to start making these rolls about three or four hours before you want to eat them. Since there's no chance you will be getting up at five in the morning, perhaps we'd better call them "afternoon rolls."

Cocoa Puff Cupcakes

The icing on the cake

There are few better-suited munchie foods than sweet cupcakes, save for cupcakes containing weed. You will need to draw on all the culinary skills you have learned so far, since you need to make both the cupcakes and a separate icing, but the rewards are obvious.

How High?:
🌿 🌿

Difficulty:
🌿 🌿 🌿

Makin' Time:
20 minutes

Bakin' Time:
20–22 minutes

Cupcakes

1 ½ cups (225 g) all-purpose flour

1 cup (200 g) sugar

½ cup (50 g) cocoa powder

1 teaspoon baking soda

¼ teaspoon salt

1 large egg

Scant 6 tablespoons (80 g) Boosted Butter (page 12), melted

2 ½ tablespoons (35 g) butter, melted

1 teaspoon vanilla extract

1 cup (240 ml) whole milk

Icing

1 cup (100 g) confectioners' sugar

1 ½ tablespoons milk

2 or 3 large handfuls Cocoa Puffs cereal

Makes 16 cupcakes

I Preheat the oven to 350°F (180°C/gas mark 4). Line muffin pans with paper baking cups. Sift the flour, sugar, cocoa, baking soda, and salt into a large bowl.

2 In another bowl, whisk the egg together with the butters and vanilla extract until well mixed. Stir the egg mixture into the flour mixture until just combined.

3 Pour into the prepared muffin pans until each cup is two-thirds full.

4 Bake for 20 to 22 minutes, until a skewer inserted into the center comes out clean. (Don't use your poker; that's unhygienic.) Allow to cool in the pans for 5 to 10 minutes; then remove the cupcakes from the pans and leave to cool completely on a wire rack.

5 To make the icing, stir the sugar and milk together in a bowl and then dribble this over the cupcakes in a spiral or zigzag pattern. Dot the cocoa puffs over the tops, arranging them in an attractive manner.

Cranberry and Walnut Bread Blast

Use your loaf

This classic bread recipe does contain a large number of ingredients, but you can make it in five quick and easy steps, giving you time to get on with the rest of your day—namely eating the bread, smoking j's, and watching reruns of "The Simpsons."

I Preheat the oven to 350°F (180°C/gas mark 4) and grease a 9 by 5-inch (23 by 12-cm) loaf pan. Mix together the flour, sugar, baking powder, salt, baking soda, and Pot Powder in a mixing bowl.

How High?:
🌿🌿🌿🌿🌿

Difficulty:
🌿🌿🌿🌿🌿

Makin' Time:
15 minutes

Bakin' Time:
55 minutes

2 cups (300 g) all-purpose flour
1 cup (200 g) granulated sugar
1 1/2 teaspoons baking powder
1 teaspoon salt
1/2 teaspoon baking soda
2 tablespoons plus 2 teaspoons Pot Powder (page 16)
3/4 cup (180 ml) orange juice

1 tablespoon grated orange zest
2 tablespoons vegetable oil
1 large egg, well beaten
1 1/2 cups (175 g) fresh or frozen cranberries, coarsely chopped
1/2 cup (55 g) chopped walnuts

Makes 1 loaf

3 Stir in the cranberries and nuts.

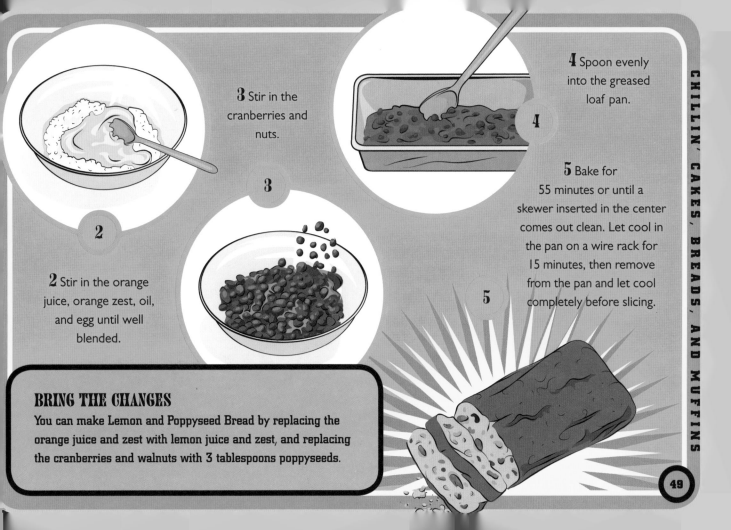

4 Spoon evenly into the greased loaf pan.

5 Bake for 55 minutes or until a skewer inserted in the center comes out clean. Let cool in the pan on a wire rack for 15 minutes, then remove from the pan and let cool completely before slicing.

2 Stir in the orange juice, orange zest, oil, and egg until well blended.

BRING THE CHANGES
You can make Lemon and Poppyseed Bread by replacing the orange juice and zest with lemon juice and zest, and replacing the cranberries and walnuts with 3 tablespoons poppyseeds.

Blueberry Blast Muffins

They're "berry" good

As American as, err, apple pie, these blueberry muffins taste mighty fine whether eaten as a civilized afternoon snack or as an accompaniment to any smoking session, and they pack a punch. Once you've made this recipe a couple of times and got your technique perfected, why not put your newfound baking skills to the test at your folks' next family get-together? It'll be a Thanksgiving to remember—well, not for Aunt Sally—she'll be stoned out of her mind—but you know what I mean.

How High?:

Difficulty:

Makin' Time:
30 minutes, plus coolin'

Bakin' Time:
20–25 minutes

3 cups [450 g] all-purpose flour

1 tablespoon baking powder

1/2 teaspoon baking soda

1/2 teaspoon salt

4 tablespoons plus 1 teaspoon [60 g] Boosted Butter [page 12]. at room temperature

6 tablespoons plus 1 teaspoon [90 g] butter. at room temperature

1 cup [200 g] sugar

2 large eggs. beaten

1 teaspoon grated lemon zest

1 1/2 cups [360 ml] plain yogurt

1 1/2 cups [350 g] fresh or frozen blueberries

Makes about 12 muffins

2 In a large mixing bowl, beating by hand or using a hand-held electric mixer, cream the butters and sugar together until fluffy.

1

2

3

I Preheat the oven to 400°F (200°C/gas mark 6). Sift the flour, baking powder, baking soda, and salt into a bowl. Set aside. We'll remind you about this later, because we know you'll forget about it otherwise.

3 Add the eggs one at a time, beating until each egg is incorporated before adding the next. Beat in the grated lemon zest.

4 Beat in half of the flour mixture until just incorporated. Then beat in one third of the yogurt. Beat in half of the remaining flour mixture, then beat in a second third of the yogurt. Beat in the remaining flour mixture followed by the remaining yogurt. In each case, be careful to beat until just incorporated but do not overbeat. There's a lot of beating involved here, as you've probably noticed. Don't wear yourself out.

5 Fold in the blueberries.

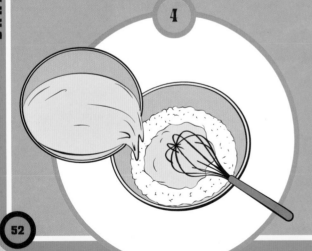

GANGA GARNISH

For a final flourish, why not sprinkle a little of your stash on the top of the cooled muffins? It'll make 'em taste all the better.

6 Lightly butter the cups of a 12-cup muffin pan. Spoon the dough into the cups. Bake for 20 to 25 minutes, about the time it takes to smoke a couple of j's, until the muffins are golden brown on top. To make sure the centers of the muffins are done, test with a long toothpick or skewer, which should come out clean.

7

6

8 Voilà, a selection of scrumptious muffins just like your mom used to make—well, aside from all the chronic you've added, obviously.

8

7 Allow the muffins to cool in the pan on a wire rack for 5 minutes; then take them out of the pan and serve slightly warm.

Mary Jane's Banana Bread

Yellow peril

Named for a famous euphemism for marijuana (great code for when you're talking to your dealer), Mary Jane's special bread works well as a between-meal hit on its own or perhaps with a mug of "herbal" tea. The potassium inherent in bananas will impart plenty of energy, so make sure you load up on the chronic to dampen any desire to go jumping around.

How High?:
🌿 🌿 🌿 🌿

Difficulty:
🌿 🌿 🌿 🌿

Makin' Time:
15 minutes

Bakin' Time:
About 1 hour

3 or 4 very ripe (or even overripe) bananas, peeled

3 tablespoons (40 g) Boosted Butter, melted

2 tablespoons plus 1 teaspoon (35 g) butter, melted

¾ cup to 1 cup (150 to 200 g) sugar (depending on how sweet you want the bread; you may be too stoned to care)

2 eggs, beaten

⅓ cup buttermilk or milk

1 teaspoon vanilla extract

1 teaspoon baking soda

Generous pinch of salt

1 ½ cups (225 g) all-purpose flour

Makes 1 loaf

I Preheat the oven to 350°F (180°C/gas mark 4) and lightly grease a 4 by 8-inch (10 by 20-cm) loaf pan.

I

SWEET TOOTH?
For an extra kick, replace half the regular butter with warmed peanut butter. Chocoholics can add a couple of handfuls of chocolate chips to the final mix before baking.

3 Using a wooden spoon, stir the butters into the mashed bananas. Then stir in the sugar, eggs, buttermilk, and vanilla extract. Sprinkle the baking soda and salt over the mixture, and stir until blended. Finally, sift in the flour and stir until blended.

2

2 Mash the bananas well in a large mixing bowl.

3

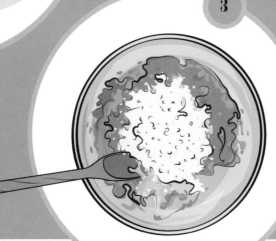

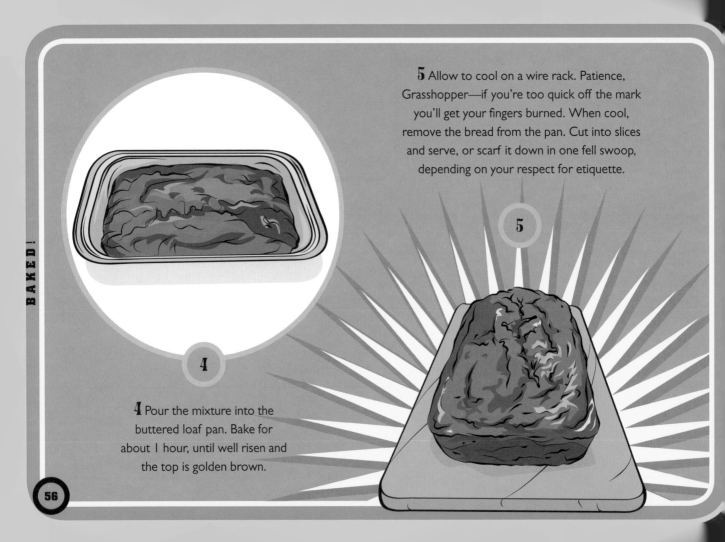

5 Allow to cool on a wire rack. Patience, Grasshopper—if you're too quick off the mark you'll get your fingers burned. When cool, remove the bread from the pan. Cut into slices and serve, or scarf it down in one fell swoop, depending on your respect for etiquette.

5

4

4 Pour the mixture into the buttered loaf pan. Bake for about 1 hour, until well risen and the top is golden brown.

Fruity Loopy Cake

Insane in the brain

Yes, it might seem like normal bread with some raisins in it, but the traditional fruit cake is a real family favorite. If you're not planning to eat your loopy cake right away, make sure it is well hidden from any non-tokin' relatives, or all hell could break loose at your mom's next brunch.

4 tablespoons plus 1 teaspoon [60 g] Boosted Butter [page 12]

2 cups [480 ml] orange juice

2 cups [400 g] sugar

2 cups [300 g] golden raisins or mixed dried fruit

1/2 cup [85 g] chopped mixed candied fruit [mixed peel]

3 cups [450 g] all-purpose flour

1 teaspoon ground ginger

1 teaspoon ground cinnamon

1 teaspoon baking soda

Makes 1 loaf

How High?:
🍁 🍁 🍁

Difficulty:
🍁 🍁 🍁

Makin' Time:
20 minutes

Bakin' Time:
45 minutes

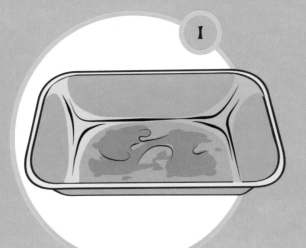

I Preheat the oven to 350°F (180°C/gas mark 4). Grease a 4 by 8-inch (10 by 20-cm) loaf pan, then flour the bottom of the pan or line it with parchment.

2

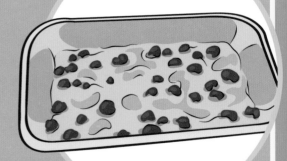

3 Remove from the heat and allow to cool for a few minutes. Stir in the flour, spices, and baking soda.

3

4

2 In a large saucepan, combine the orange juice, sugar, raisins, candied fruit, and Boosted Butter, and heat gently over a low heat until the butter melts and the sugar dissolves. This will smell real nice, but concentrate, because there is work to be done.

4 Pour into the prepared loaf pan and bake for 45 minutes or until a skewer inserted into the cake's center comes out clean.

5 Remove from the oven and let cool in the pan for about 10 minutes; then turn out on a wire rack to cool further.

5

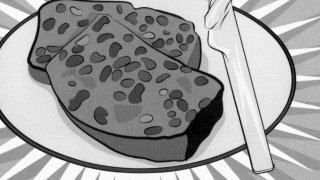

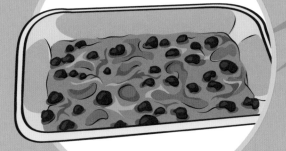

6

6 Cut into slices and serve with butter. The slices are also delicious toasted and buttered.

chapter 4

PIPIN' PASTRIES AND BROWNIES

"Taste the hashish, guest of mine—taste the hashish.

"The Count of Monte Cristo," Alexandre Dumas

Pastries are the high art of the baker, but they don't have to be daunting. What you need is patience, a large bong bowl for while the confections are chilling in the fridge, cool hands, and a light touch. Whenever possible, avoid adding too much water to a dough or too much flour when you are rolling it out, because both will make your pastry tough.

Bender Bars

Get your oats

Have you been bitten by the cooking bug yet? No? Then get ready for some Bender Bars. With a generous dose of oats and dried fruit, these bakes contain plenty of fiber to keep you regular and lots of sugar to give you energy. If it weren't for the Boosted Butter, this recipe could grace any "straight" cookbook, but we wouldn't want to lose that, would we?

How High?:
❋ ❋ ❋ ❋ ❋

Difficulty:
❋ ❋ ❋ ❋ ❋

Makin' Time:
25 minutes

Bakin' Time:
About 30 minutes

Crust

Scant ½ cup plus ½ teaspoon (100 g) Boosted Butter (page 12)

Scant ½ cup plus ½ teaspoon (100 g) butter

½ cup (100 g) firmly packed brown sugar

¾ cup (180 ml) maple syrup

½ cup (75 g) all-purpose flour

2 ¾ cups (240 g) rolled oats

½ cup (75 g) dried fruit, such as raisins, cranberries, or raspberries, or a combination of these

Caramel topping

2 tablespoons heavy cream

¼ cup (55 g) butter

½ cup (100 g) firmly packed brown sugar

Makes about 20 bars

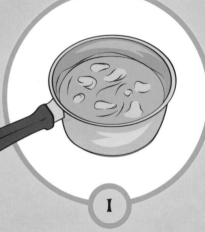

I

I Preheat the oven to 350°F (180°C/gas mark 4). In a large, heavy saucepan over very low heat, combine the butters, sugar, and syrup, stirring to make sure nothing sticks and burns, until the butter and sugar have melted completely.

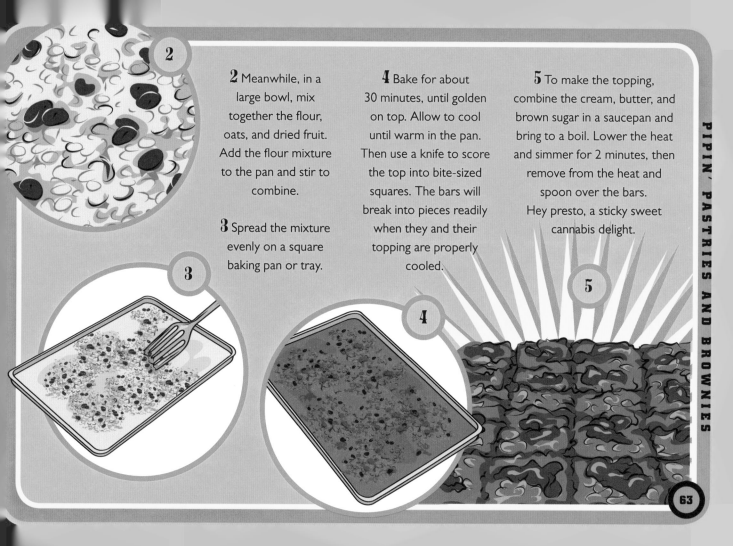

2 Meanwhile, in a large bowl, mix together the flour, oats, and dried fruit. Add the flour mixture to the pan and stir to combine.

3 Spread the mixture evenly on a square baking pan or tray.

4 Bake for about 30 minutes, until golden on top. Allow to cool until warm in the pan. Then use a knife to score the top into bite-sized squares. The bars will break into pieces readily when they and their topping are properly cooled.

5 To make the topping, combine the cream, butter, and brown sugar in a saucepan and bring to a boil. Lower the heat and simmer for 2 minutes, then remove from the heat and spoon over the bars. Hey presto, a sticky sweet cannabis delight.

Blackout Buns

Zero recall

This recipe contains three separate elements—dough, filling, and glaze—but don't flee the kitchen in panic. Making these buns is more straightforward than it seems. Put the hard work in now and follow these nine steps to success—there'll be plenty of time for sleeping/unconsciousness once you've eaten them.

How High?:

Difficulty:

Makin' Time:
30 minutes, plus 2 hours risin' and coolin'

Bakin' Time:
45–60 minutes

Dough

4 cups (600 g) all-purpose flour

1 ¼ cups (300 ml) warm milk

2 teaspoons quick-rising active dry yeast

2 tablespoons (27.5 g) Boosted Butter (page 12). melted

¼ cup (50 g) sugar

1 teaspoon salt

1 tablespoon finely grated orange zest

Filling

1 cup (170 g) seedless raisins or currants

2 tablespoons plus 1 teaspoon (32.5 g) Boosted Butter (page 12). melted

1 tablespoon plus 2 teaspoons (27.5 g) butter. melted

½ cup (100 g) firmly packed brown sugar

1 teaspoon ground cinnamon

1 teaspoon pumpkin pie spice

½ cup (60 g) chopped walnuts

Glaze

1 cup (120 g) confectioners' sugar

1 tablespoon lemon juice

Makes 12 buns

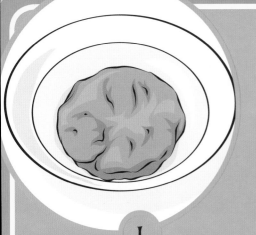

1

I To make the dough, stir together all of the dough ingredients in a large bowl and then knead until smooth, 5 to 10 minutes. The dough should be tacky but not sticky. If it is too moist add a little extra flour. Place the dough in another large ungreased bowl, cover, and set aside in a warm place to rise until doubled in size, about 1 hour. Lightly butter a baking sheet.

2 Meanwhile, plump up the raisins for the filling: place them in a small bowl, pour very hot water over them, and let them soak in the water for about 15 minutes before draining. This will keep them moist during baking.

3

2

3 To make the filling, stir together the melted butters, brown sugar, and spices in a small bowl.

65

4 When the dough has risen, roll it out on a floured surface until about 1/4 inch (0.5 cm) thick.

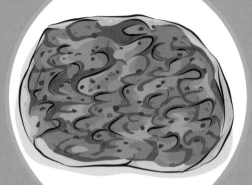

5

6 Roll the dough up around the filling lengthwise as you would with a jelly roll, trying to prevent the filling from spilling out. Then slice the roll crosswise into 12 even pieces.

6

4

5 Spread the filling on the risen dough and sprinkle the drained raisins and walnut pieces over the top.

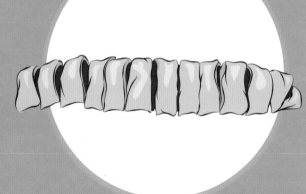

8 Bake the risen buns for 20 to 25 minutes until nicely golden. Let the rolls cool for about 20 minutes on the pan.

7

7 Place the pieces close together on the lightly buttered baking sheet. Cover with a cloth and let the buns rise for another 45 minutes to an hour, until roughly doubled in size. Preheat the oven to 375°F (190°C/gas mark 5). Go and have a smoke, you've earned a break.

8

9

9 In a small bowl, stir together the confectioners' sugar and lemon juice and drizzle it over the buns. Allow the buns to cool further and the glaze to set. Eat and prepare for the blackout.

67

Zigzag pastries

Shapeshifting

Are you feeling the pressure? Good. Here's another great pastry recipe to test your kitchen prowess. Getting the pastry shape right on this one can be a bit tricky for culinary virgins, so tackle it while sober to guarantee success. The end result looks mighty fine and tastes even better.

How High?:

Difficulty:

Makin' Time:
About 1 hour, plus 10–10$^{1/2}$ hours of chillin' and risin'

Bakin' Time:
12 minutes

Pastry

4 1/2 tablespoons warm water

Generous 1 3/4 teaspoons quick-rising active dry yeast

Scant 1/2 cup whole milk, at room temperature

1 large egg, at room temperature

1/4 cup (50 g) sugar

1 teaspoon salt

Scant 2 1/4 cups (336 g) all-purpose flour

5 tablespoons plus 2 teaspoons (80 g) Boosted Butter (page 12), chilled, cut into 1/4-inch (5-mm) slices

1/2 cup plus 1 tablespoon and 2 teaspoons (145 g) butter, chilled, cut into 1/4-inch (5-mm) slices

Almond filling

3 tablespoons all-purpose flour

2/3 cup (100 g) finely ground blanched almonds

3 1/2 tablespoons butter, at room temperature

3 1/2 tablespoons sugar

1 egg, lightly beaten, at room temperature

2/3 teaspoon rum

1 egg, lightly beaten

Fresh fruit, such as grapes, pitted cherries, blueberries, strawberries, or apricot halves, etc.

Makes 16 pastries

1 The day before you want to eat it, make the pastry. In a large bowl, whisk together the warm water and yeast. Let stand for a minute, and then whisk in the milk, egg, sugar, and salt and set aside. Place the flour in the bowl of a food processor (or use a pastry blender or a knife in a bowl). Pulse the processor briefly about 10 times, until the butter is cut into pieces about 1/2-inch (1-cm) diameter. Don't overprocess!

2 Add the flour and butter mixture to the milk mixture. Fold with a spatula until the liquid ingredients are just barely incorporated. The dough will be very rough and chunky with butter. Cover the bowl and chill the dough for at least 8 hours.

3 Turn the dough out on a floured surface, sprinkle it lightly with flour, and pat it into a rough square shape. Roll the dough into a 16-inch (40-cm) square. Fold it into thirds, as you would a letter. Roll the folded dough again into a 24 by 10-inch (60 by 25-cm) rectangle. Again fold the dough in thirds so you have a 8 by 10-inch (20 by 25-cm) rectangle. Wrap it in plastic and chill for about 45 minutes. Repeat the above process of rolling and folding twice, finishing with an 8 by 10-inch (20 by 25-cm) rectangle. Wrap in plastic again and chill for 30 minutes.

4

4 While the pastry chills, make the filling. In a small bowl, combine the flour and ground almonds together. With a hand-held electric mixer in another bowl, cream together the butter and sugar. Add the egg a little at a time, beating well on medium speed after each addition. Beat until light and fluffy. Add the flour mixture and beat until well combined. Stir in the rum.

5 To make the pastries, line 2 baking sheets with parchment. Cut the chilled dough in half to make two rectangles. While working with the first half, keep the other in the fridge. On a floured surface, roll the first piece of dough into a 20 by 10-inch (50 by 25-cm) rectangle. Trim the rectangle just enough to give it clean edges. Using a sharp knife pressed firmly down into the dough, cut the dough into 8 pieces, each 5 inches (12.5 cm) square. Do not drag the knife through the dough, as this makes the layers stick together. On each piece, make diagonal cuts in from each corner halfway to the center, as shown.

6 Fold the left-hand side of each quarter into the center to make a pinwheel as shown.

5

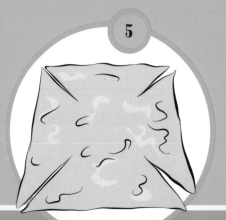

6

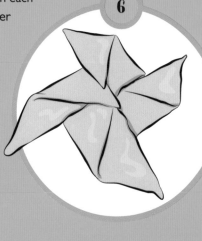

7 Place the pieces on the parchment-lined baking sheets. Brush the tops lightly with egg, avoiding the cut edges of the dough, as this tends to glue them together. Repeat with the other half of the dough. Cover with plastic wrap or slip into a large plastic bag, and refrigerate over-night. In the morning, remove the pastries from the refrigerator and let them rise, still covered, for about 1 1/2 to 2 hours, until they feel light and puffy.

7

8 Preheat the oven to 375°F (190°C/gas mark 5). Brush the pastries again with egg. With wet fingers, make a depression in the center of each pastry. Fill with about one tablespoon of filling, and press some fruit into the filling. Bake for about 12 minutes, until nicely risen and well colored.

8

EASIER THAN IT LOOKS

Making this sort of pastry may look very difficult, but it isn't really—it is just lengthy, involving lots of rolling and resting in the refrigerator (the pastry, that is, not you!). You'll also see that you really need to make and shape the pastry a day ahead of baking, which is very brief.

Toker's Treacle Tartlets

Sweet-toothed treat

A traditional British version of shoofly pie, these treacle tarts require you to make both a shortcrust pastry and a filling pretty much at the same time. If you can coordinate your stoned mind to do all this, then maybe you should consider extending your dalliance with the kitchen stove and doing some complex "straight" cooking as well. Then again . . .

I To make the filling, place all the ingredients for the filling in a large bowl and stir until well combined. Cover and refrigerate for at least one hour.

How High?:
✹ ✹ ✹ ✹

Difficulty:
✹ ✹ ✹ ✹ ✹

Makin' Time:
30 minutes, plus
1½ hours chillin'

Bakin' Time:
20–25 minutes

Filling

1 ⅓ cups (450 g) light treacle or golden syrup

1 cup (115 g) fine white breadcrumbs

Finely grated zest of 1 lemon

2 teaspoons lemon juice

⅔ cup (165 ml) heavy cream

2 eggs, beaten

3 ounces (80 g) ground almonds

Shortcrust pastry

2 ½ cups (375 g) all-purpose flour, plus additional for rolling

1 teaspoon salt

2 tablespoons sugar

½ cup plus 1 teaspoon (120 g) Boosted Butter (page 12), chilled and cut into cubes

Scant ½ cup plus 1 ½ teaspoons (105 g) butter, chilled and cut into cubes

1 egg, beaten

Makes 24 little tartlets

2 To make the pastry, in a medium bowl (or in a food processor) combine the flour, salt, and sugar. Add the butters and beat (or pulse) until the dough is coarse and crumbly.

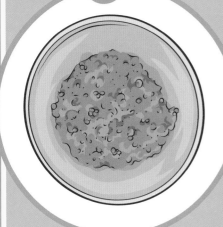

4 On a floured board, roll the chilled dough out to a rectangle about 22 by 14 inches (55 by 35 cm) and cut it into 24 (4-inch, or 10-cm) circles using a large, round cutter or a knife and a suitably sized glass, rerolling the pastry trimmings if necessary. Place the rounds in muffin tin(s) and chill in the refrigerator for about 30 minutes.

3 Add the beaten egg and beat until a dough forms. Wrap it in plastic wrap and refrigerate for at least one hour.

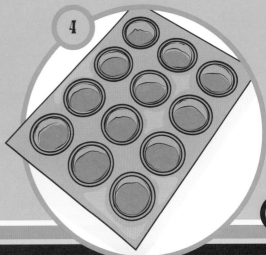

6 Remove from the oven, allow to cool, and serve. Then wait for the tartlets to work their magic.

5 When ready to cook, preheat the oven to 375°F (190°C/gas mark 5). Spoon the filling into the tartlet cases and bake for 20 to 25 minutes, or until the pastry has browned nicely.

WANT THAT WITH CREAM?

These little nuggets of sweet delight look and taste even better if topped with a spoonful of fresh whipped cream, thick crème fraîche, or ice cream.

Hash Brownies

A stoner's staple diet

I

This cannabis cookery classic, widely available in legalized coffee shops around the world, can be made with hash or grass. You can vary this basic recipe with several possible additions to the finished batter: try 2 cups (225 g) chopped toasted pecans or walnuts or 1½ cups (255 g) chocolate chips. But, frankly, as long as you've got a good dose of chronic in there, who cares?

How High?:
🌿 🌿 🌿

Difficulty:
🌿 🌿 🌿

Makin' Time:
30 minutes

Bakin' Time:
35 minutes

6 ounces (170 g) high-quality unsweetened chocolate, coarsely chopped

½ cup plus 1 teaspoon (120 g) Boosted Butter, cut into chunks

¼ cup (50 g) butter, cut into small chunks

¾ teaspoon salt

2 cups (400 g) granulated sugar

3 large eggs

1 teaspoon vanilla extract

1 cup (150 g) all-purpose flour

Makes about 24 brownies

I Place a rack in the center position in the oven and preheat to 325°F (160°C/gas mark 3). Butter a 9 by 13-inch (23 by 32-cm) pan, and then dust it with flour or cocoa powder. Put the chocolate and butter in a large metal bowl set over a pan of simmering water; the bowl should not touch the water.

2

CHOCO TIPS

Chocolate melts fairly easily, but it can burn when heated too high. Melting it over steam is an easy way to keep the temperature at a moderate level. Be careful not to introduce steam directly into the chocolate because this can also cause the melted chocolate to separate.

3 In a small bowl, lightly beat the eggs and vanilla extract together. Add this to the chocolate mixture and stir until the eggs are well blended into the chocolate. Add the flour to the batter and stir until all the flour is incorporated.

3

2 Stir gently while the chocolate and the butters melt (mmm, smell that). When all is melted, turn off the heat but keep the bowl over the hot water to keep the mixture warm and easy to work with. Stir to mix the butter and chocolate together well. Add the salt and sugar and stir.

4 Pour the batter into the prepared baking pan. The batter will be fairly thick, so you may need to help spread it with a spatula. Bake for 35–40 minutes on the center rack in the oven.

4

SMALL IS BEAUTIFUL

Using a smaller pan, such as an 8-inch (20-cm) square one, will produce thicker and chewier brownies. The baking time may need to be increased to achieve the desired texture.

5 Remove from the oven and allow to cool in the pan before cutting the brownies into 2-inch (5-cm) squares. Gather your smoking buddies and dig in.

5

IS IT READY?

To check if the brownies are done, insert a skewer into the center of the brownie. It should come out with small brownie crumbs on it and no batter. (If it comes out totally clean, then you may have overbaked it—doh!)

Whities

Lightweights beware

These delicious cakes are named for their light-colored appearance (courtesy of the white chocolate) rather than for the pale-skin affliction that affects lightweight tokers but, needless to say, if you consume too many of these cakes, you will likely be vulnerable to just that problem. Proceed with caution.

I Preheat the oven to 350°F (180°C/gas mark 4). Butter and flour an 8-inch (20-cm) square baking pan or line it with foil. Melt the Boosted Butter and 4 ounces (115 g) of the white chocolate together in a metal bowl set over a pan of simmering water; the bowl should not touch the water. When they have melted, remove the bowl from the heat and add the remaining white chocolate. Stir to blend well and set aside.

How High?:

Difficulty:

Makin' Time:
25 minutes

Bakin' Time:
About 35 minutes

¼ cup plus 2 tablespoons (85 g) Boosted Butter (page 12)

8 ounces (225 g) white chocolate, coarsely chopped

2 eggs

¼ cup (50 g) sugar

1 ½ teaspoons vanilla extract

1 cup (150 g) all-purpose flour

Pinch of salt

½ teaspoon baking powder

3 ½ teaspoons Pot Powder (page 16)

½ cup (85 g) dark chocolate chips

Makes about 24 squares

CHERRY AID
Make these into Bleeding Hearties by replacing the dark chocolate chips with chopped candied cherries.

78

2

2 In a large bowl, beat the eggs and sugar until pale and thick.

3 Add the white chocolate and butter mixture, vanilla extract, flour, salt, baking powder, and Pot Powder. Beat just until smooth.

3

4

4 Stir in the chocolate chips, being careful not to overmix.

5 You may be tempted to sit down and gorge on the batter, but resist. Instead, pour it into the prepared pan and bake for 35 minutes or until a skewer inserted in the center comes out clean. Let cool in the pan.

5

6

6 Cut into squares and serve to your stoner buddies.

chapter 5

SPARKIN' SWEET TREATS

"The pursuit of perfection, then, is the pursuit of sweetness and light."

Matthew Arnold

This chapter is all about ways of enjoying the deliciously different textures that sugar can give baked goods, from the gloriously gooey to the captivatingly crunchy. Be careful, though, when handling things like caramel, syrups, and hot cooked sugar as they really pack a lot of heat, and can burn you badly if you get splashed.

Chunky Caramel Bars

Dope delight

Packed with calories—oats, sugar, chocolate—for energy, these caramel bars have a healthy cannabis content that serves as a balancing ingredient. So, while certain other brands of snack bar are designed to get you active, these marijuana-laden munchies will just make you rest . . . a lot.

How High?:
✳ ✳ ✳ ✳ ✳

Difficulty:
✳ ✳ ✳ ✳ ✳

Makin' Time:
25 minutes, plus
10 minutes' coolin'

Bakin' Time:
30–34 minutes

1 ¾ cups (150 g) rolled oats

1 ½ cups (225 g) all-purpose flour

¾ cup (150 g) firmly packed brown sugar

½ teaspoon baking soda

¼ teaspoon salt

¼ cup plus 5 teaspoons (80 g) Boosted Butter (see page 12), melted

¼ cup plus 3 tablespoons (95 g) butter, melted

Caramel topping

½ cup (100 g) firmly packed brown sugar

½ cup (100 g) granulated sugar

½ cup (115 g) butter

¼ cup (37 g) all-purpose flour

1 cup (125 g) chopped mixed nuts

1 cup (175 g) chocolate, chopped

Makes 16 bars

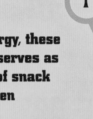

I Preheat the oven to 375°F (200°C/gas mark 6) and lightly grease a 13 by 9-inch (33 by 23-cm) baking pan. In a large mixing bowl, combine the oats, flour, brown sugar, baking soda, and salt; mix well. Add the butters and stir until crumbly. Measure 1 cup (150 g) of the mixture for the topping; set aside.

TOP THAT
For an extra kick, stir in a teaspoon of Boosted Butter when preparing the topping.

2 Press the remaining oat mixture into the bottom of the prepared pan. Bake for 10 to 12 minutes, until light golden brown. Remove from the oven and let cool for 10 minutes (don't turn off the oven yet.)

3

3 Meanwhile, to make the caramel topping, stir the sugars and butter together in a heavy pan. Heat over low heat until bubbling and let simmer gently for 1 minute. Remove from the heat and let cool until tepid; then stir in the flour until smooth.

4 Top the cooled oat base with the nut and chocolate pieces. Drizzle the caramel topping over these to within 1/4 inch (5 mm) of the edge. Sprinkle with the reserved uncooked oat mix and pat this gently into the caramel. Bake for a further 20 to 22 minutes until golden brown all over.

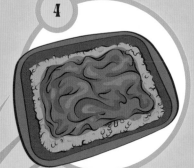

4

5 Leave to cool completely, and cut into bars. Nutty but nice.

5

Chocolate Fingers

Finger lickin' good

Another sweet treat, these chocolate fingers are a delight to make and eat. They're tricky to roll well and may require some practice, but if you mess up you can always eat them and make another batch. Hooray! Don't eat a whole handful at once.

I

How High?:
🍁🍁🍁🍁🍁

Difficulty:
🍁🍁🍁🍁

Makin' Time:
30 minutes, plus
10 minutes' coolin'

Bakin' Time:
12–15 minutes

7 ounces (200 g) dark chocolate. broken into pieces
3 tablespoons plus 2 teaspoons (50 g) Boosted Butter (page 12). at room temperature
5 tablespoons (65 g) butter. at room temperature
1/2 cup (60 g) confectioner's sugar
1 1/4 cups (187 g) self-rising flour
3 tablespoons cornstarch
1/2 teaspoon vanilla extract

Makes about 10 fingers

I Preheat the oven to 375°F (190°C/gas mark 5) and lightly butter 2 baking sheets. Melt 3 ounces (75 g) of the dark chocolate in a heatproof bowl set over but not touching a pan of simmering water. Remove from heat and allow to cool, but don't get a spoon and eat it.

GET SOME NUTS!
You can add extra flavor to these fingers by adding finely chopped walnuts with the vanilla extract.

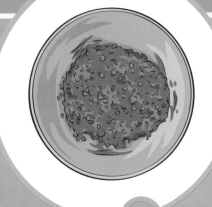

2 In a large mixing bowl, using a hand-held electric mixer, beat the butters until smooth; then beat in the sugar and the cooled, but still liquid, chocolate.

4 Lightly flour your hands as necessary. Spooning out a handful at a time, compress the mixture into a ball and carefully roll it into a finger or cigar shape about 2¹/₂ inches (6 cm) long. Arrange on the prepared baking sheets, spaced well apart to allow for spreading. Run the prongs of a warmed fork along each finger to decorate it.

3 Sift in the flour and cornstarch. Beat well, adding the vanilla extract.

5 Bake in the preheated oven for 12 to 15 minutes, until a toothpick inserted into the middle of one finger comes out clean. Leave them to cool slightly on the baking sheets, then transfer them very carefully to wire racks and leave to cool completely.

6

5

6 Melt the remaining chocolate and dip one end of each finger in the chocolate, allowing excess to drip back into the bowl. Place the fingers on a sheet of baking parchment and leave to set.

7 Eat and be merry.

7

JOINT EFFORT
Use white chocolate and strawberry sauce to give your fingers the appearance of a roaring reefer. Neat.

Morning Meltdown

Daytime dreamin'

This is a baked version of the breakfast classic, French toast. It lends itself to all sorts of variations (see box on page 88) but all of these variations feature the secret ingredient to ensure your day ends before it's really begun. Since you have to make it about 9 hours before you want to serve it, it is best made before you go to bed and then baked in the morning . . . or whenever you eventually rise from your slumber.

How High?:
✹ ✹ ✹ ✹

Difficulty:
✹ ✹ ✹ ✹ ✹

Makin' Time:
20 minutes, plus
8 hours chillin'

Bakin' Time:
45–55 minutes

1 (16-ounce/450-g)
French baguette

3 tablespoons (40 g)
Boosted Butter
(page 12), at room
temperature

1 1/2 tablespoons (20 g)
butter, at room
temperature

4 large eggs

1 cup (240 ml) milk

1/4 cup (50 g) sugar

3 or 4 tablespoons
maple syrup

1 teaspoon vanilla
extract

1/2 teaspoon salt

Confectioners'
sugar (optional)

Makes 8 slices

1 At least 9 hours before you want to serve, ideally the night before, lightly butter a 13 by 9-inch (32.5 by 23-cm) baking dish. Cut the baguette crosswise at an angle into about 8 slices each about 3/4 inch (2 cm) thick.

2 In a small bowl, cream the two butters together until combined. Spread one side of each slice with an equal portion of the mixed butter. Arrange the slices, buttered side up, in the prepared baking dish.

3 Whisk together the eggs with the milk, sugar, maple syrup, vanilla extract, and salt.

3

4

4 Pour this mixture over the bread and press the slices down into it. Tip the dish and spoon the egg mixture over the bread slices as much as you can. Cover and chill for about 8 hours. Now you can go get really wasted.

FRESH TWIST

You can make this richer by using cream instead of milk, or add a large handful of golden raisins (sultanas) or other dried fruit. Or, instead of the maple syrup, use a teaspoon each of freshly grated nutmeg and ground cinnamon.

5 When ready to cook, preheat the oven to 350°F (180°C/gas mark 4). Put the baking dish, uncovered, in the preheated oven for 45 to 55 minutes, until the top is nicely golden.

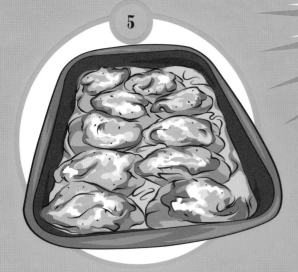

5

6

6 If you like, dust lightly with confectioners' sugar just before serving. Yummy.

Sticky Ickies

Gooey ganja delight

It's not cooking these sugary morsels that you'll find challenging, it's eating them—they're not called sticky ickies for nothing. So when it's time for bed, put them out of harm's way. Don't be the one to wake at four in the morning with one stuck to your forehead.

How High?:
🌿 🌿 🌿 🌿

Difficulty:
🌿 🌿 🌿 🌿 🌿

Makin' Time:
30 minutes

Bakin' Time:
25–35 minutes

1/2 cup (120 ml) light corn syrup or maple syrup

2/3 cup (65 g) firmly packed brown sugar

1/2 cup plus 1 teaspoon (60 g) Boosted Butter (page 12), chilled and cut into cubes

1/2 cup (115 g) butter, chilled and cut into cubes

1/3 cup (50 g) coarsely chopped pecans or walnuts

1/2 cup (80 g) chopped dates

4 cups (600 g) self-rising flour

1 teaspoon salt

1 1/2 cups (360 ml) milk

1/2 cup (100 g) granulated sugar

1 teaspoon ground cinnamon

Makes 12 rolls

1

I Preheat the oven to 425°F (220°C/gas mark 7). In a saucepan, combine the syrup, brown sugar, 3 table-spoons (40 g) of the Boosted Butter, and I tablespoon water. Stir over low heat just until the sugar has dissolved; do not allow the mixture to boil.

2 Spread the mixture in the bottom of a 9 by 9 by 2-inch (23 by 23 by 5-cm) baking pan. Sprinkle the nuts and dates over the top.

3

2

3 Sift the flour into a large mixing bowl. Cut in the remaining butters until the mixture resembles coarse crumbs. Make a well in the center and add the milk all at once, stirring just until the dough comes together.

4 Turn the dough out onto a lightly floured surface and knead gently for a minute or two. Cut the dough in half and roll one half out into a 12 by 10-inch (30 by 25-cm) rectangle.

4

BAKED!

5 In a small bowl, combine the granulated sugar and cinnamon and sprinkle half of this over the dough.

7 Cut this crosswise into 1-inch (2.5-cm) slices. Place these, cut side down, in the prepared pan. Repeat with the rest of the dough and sugar mixture to finish covering the pan.

5

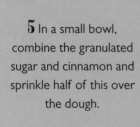

6

6 Starting from one long side, roll up the dough like a jelly roll. Keep a straight line there, now.

7

8 Bake in the preheated oven for 25 to 35 minutes until uniformly golden on top.

9 Take out of the oven and let cool slightly. Loosen the sides and tip the whole thing out on a serving plate. Serve warm.

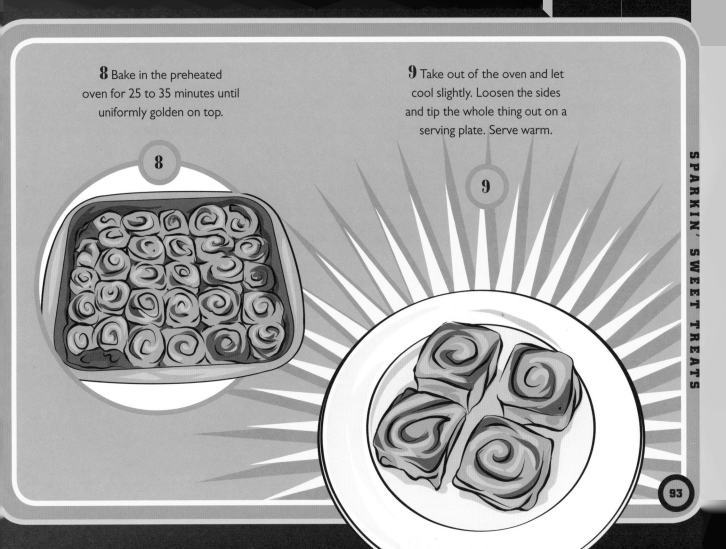

Bong Bites

Movie munchies

Nothing will stimulate your salivary glands like a taste of these miniature doughnuts, although they're not for the diet conscious. They're a buttery, sugary delight, perfect to share during a night in with your favorite Cheech and Chong movie. All together now! "Dave? Dave's not here, man."

How High?:
🌿🌿🌿🌿🌿

Difficulty:
🌿🌿🌿🌿🌿

Makin' Time:
30 minutes, plus about 1 1/2 hours risin'

Bakin' Time:
12–17 minutes

Dough

1 cup (240 ml) whole milk

3/4 cup (150 g) sugar

1 teaspoon salt

1/3 cup (75 g) Boosted Butter (page 12), cut into chunks

2 packages active dry yeast

2 eggs, at room temperature, lightly beaten

4 1/2 to 5 cups (675 to 750 g) all-purpose flour, sifted

1 teaspoon ground cinnamon

1/2 teaspoon freshly grated nutmeg

2 1/2 teaspoons Pot Powder (page 16)

Topping

3/4 cup (175 g) melted butter

1 cup (200 g) sugar

2 tablespoons ground cinnamon

Makes about 20 bites

I Scald the milk by gently bringing it to just below boiling over medium heat. Immediately turn off the heat and stir in the sugar, salt, and Boosted Butter until well combined. Allow to cool to lukewarm.

I

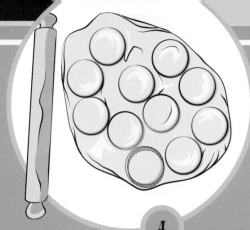

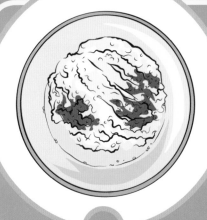

2 Pour ¹/₂ cup (120 ml) warm water into a large warmed bowl. Sprinkle in the yeast and stir until dissolved. Add the lukewarm milk mixture, the eggs, 2 cups (225 g) of the flour, the cinnamon, nutmeg, and the Pot Powder. Stir until combined.

3 Stir in just enough of the remaining flour to make a soft dough. Cover and let rise in a warm place for 50 to 60 minutes.

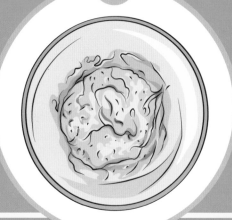

4 Lightly butter a baking sheet. Punch the dough down, turn it out on a well-floured board, and roll out to a thickness of about ¹/₂ inch (1.25 cm). Using a 3-inch (7.5-cm) round pastry cutter, cut out about 20 disks and place on the prepared baking sheet. Cover and leave to rise in a warm place for about 30 minutes.

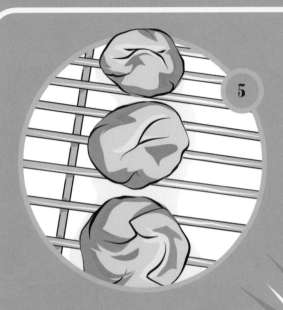

5 Preheat the oven to 400°F (200°C/gas mark 6). Brush the risen doughnuts with some of the melted butter and bake for 12 to 17 minutes until golden brown. Remove from the baking sheet and place on a wire rack to cool slightly.

6 Combine the sugar and cinnamon in a small bowl. To finish, dip the still-warm doughnuts in the remaining melted butter and then coat with the sugar mixture. Serve warm. Heaven.

NUTTY APPLE

You can give added flavor to these baked doughnuts by adding some chopped walnuts or grated apple to the mix.

Twisted Treats

Get screwed up

Bored of cooking the conventional? These puff pastry treats come with a twist, literally, and taste mighty fine. Best eaten while listening to some experimental psychedelic music, they're guaranteed to mangle your mind.

How High?:

Difficulty:

Makin' Time:
30 minutes

Bakin' Time:
18–20 minutes

2 teaspoons (10 g) butter, melted

3 tablespoons plus 2 teaspoons (50 g) Boosted Butter (page 12), melted

2 egg yolks

1 tablespoon milk

1/3 cup (75 g) sugar

1/2 teaspoon ground cinnamon

1 teaspoon ground cardamon

1 (17.3-ounce) package chilled puff pastry, preferably all-butter, thawed if frozen

1/2 cup finely chopped dry-roasted pistachios

Makes about 10 twists

1 Preheat the oven to 400°F (205°C/gas mark 6) and lightly butter 2 baking sheets with a small amount of the butter. In a small bowl, stir together the two butters until combined. In another small bowl, lightly beat the egg yolks with the milk. In yet another small bowl, combine the sugar with the spices. On a lightly floured work surface, roll the puff pastry out into two 8 by 11-inch (18 by 36-cm) rectangles about 1/4 inch (5 mm) thick. Brush each sheet with the egg wash and then sprinkle them evenly with a tablespoon each of the sugar mixture.

1

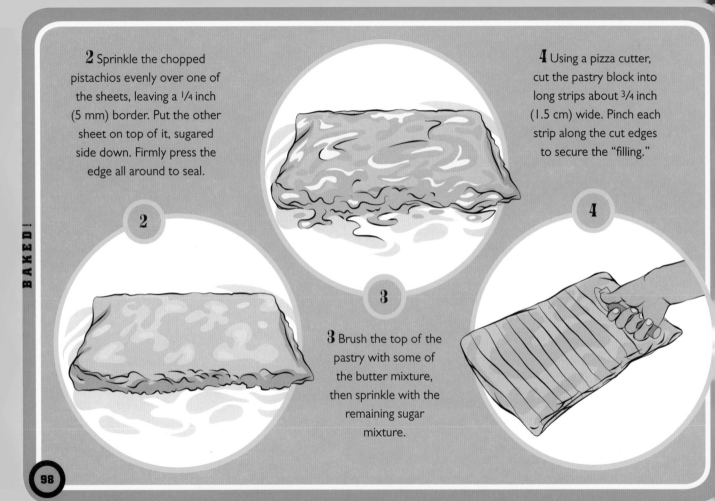

2 Sprinkle the chopped pistachios evenly over one of the sheets, leaving a ¼ inch (5 mm) border. Put the other sheet on top of it, sugared side down. Firmly press the edge all around to seal.

2

4 Using a pizza cutter, cut the pastry block into long strips about ¾ inch (1.5 cm) wide. Pinch each strip along the cut edges to secure the "filling."

4

3

3 Brush the top of the pastry with some of the butter mixture, then sprinkle with the remaining sugar mixture.

5 Twist each strip 3 times, trying to ensure that the pinched edges stay together, and place them well apart on the prepared baking sheets. Brush again with the remaining butter mixture.

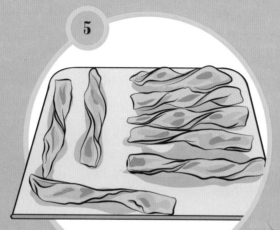

6 Bake for 18 to 20 minutes or until golden. Remove from the baking sheets immediately, and allow to cool on wire racks before eating. Twist and shout . . . and scream.

NOT HIGH ENOUGH?

If you want to make your own pastry rather than use ready made, the pastry described on pages 68–69 will work fairly well. And, of course, that way you can really boost the Boosted Butter content.

chapter 6

SALIVATIN' SAVORY BAKES

"And one went out into the field to gather herbs, and found a wild vine, and gathered thereof wild gourds his lap full, and came and shred them into the pot of pottage: for they knew them not."

The Bible (2 Kings 4:39)

Just in case you get tired of sweet bakes, presented here are a few satisfyingly savory means of getting smashed. There's something for all occasions, from snacks on toast and simple lunches to dinner party appetizers and picnic fare—even a way of packing everyone's favorite, pizza, with more than its usual pizzazz!

Phyllo Baggies

Pot parcels

These tasty morsels may look complicated to make, but they'll be a breeze for a burgeoning canna-chef like you. The buttery, crispy phyllo pastry is divine and the delicious cheese, pear, and pine nut filling forms the basis of a meal that will be both unforgettable and worryingly hard to recall.

How High?:
🌿🌿🌿🌿🌿

Difficulty:
🌿🌿🌿🌿🌿

Makin' Time:
30 minutes, plus 30 minutes chillin'

Bakin' Time:
15–20 minutes

½ cup (60 g) pine nuts

2 ripe pears, peeled, cored, and diced small

2 tablespoons honey

Juice of 1 lemon

19 ½-ounce (270-g) package filo pastry (about 12 sheets measuring 9 by 10 inches/23 by 25 cm)

¼ cup plus 5 teaspoons (80 g) Boosted Butter (page 12), melted

5 ½ ounces (150 g) gorgonzola (or other strong blue cheese), cut into small cubes

Freshly ground black pepper

Makes about 16 baggies

I To make the filling, toast the pine nuts in a dry frying pan over low to moderate heat, stirring frequently, until nicely browned. Take off the heat and stir in the pears, honey, and lemon juice. Leave to cool and then drain well.

I

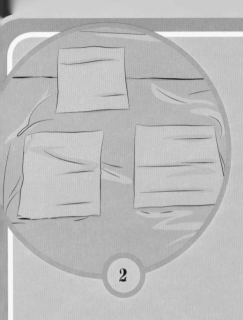

3 Brush your first piece with melted Boosted Butter, put the second piece on top of that at an angle, so the points start looking like the petals of a flower or the points of a star (aah . . .). Brush the second piece with melted butter and then do the same with a third.

2

3

4

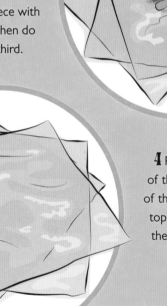

2 Make the phyllo parcels one by one, keeping the sheets of pastry not being worked with under a damp cloth so they don't dry out. Divide each sheet of phyllo pastry into rough quarters so they are approximately 5 inches (13 cm) square.

4 Put about 2 teaspoons of the cheese in the middle of the pastry "star" and then top this with a spoonful of the drained pear and pine nut mixture.

5

6 Repeat this process with the rest of the pastry and filling; you should be able to make 16 of them. Chill them for about 30 minutes.

6

5 Now comes the tricky part. Gather up the sides of the pastry and twist them together at the top gently, so they form a purse shape, pinching to secure everything in place. As you work, try to tease out the top parts of the phyllo edges so they look decorative. Place on a baking sheet lined with parchment paper.

8 Start munching on the baggies while they're still warm.

8

7

7 Preheat the oven to 400°F (200°C/gas mark 6). Bake the pastries for 15 to 20 minutes, until golden brown.

Baked! Potatoes

Pots with pot

It's likely you've baked potatoes before (in the microwave with some baked beans, at two in the morning), but much more can be achieved with the humble potato than this. So take advantage of your newfound culinary skills and try any one of these delicious fillings. As a midnight snack to get your salivary glands dancing, it's hard to beat.

How High?:

Difficulty:

Makin' Time:
15 minutes

Bakin' Time:
1¼–1¾ hours

4 large baking potatoes, each about 8 to 10 ounces (225 to 275 g), thoroughly washed and dried well ahead of cooking

Olive oil

Coarse sea salt

Freshly ground black pepper

4 teaspoons (20 g) Boosted Butter (page 12)

¼ cup (60 g) butter

Filling

Choose any of the following:

Sour cream mixed with lots of minced chives

Cottage cheese mixed with crumbled cooked bacon

Grated aged Cheddar with chopped green onions

Tuna mixed with mayonnaise

Serves 4

I Preheat the oven to 375°F (190°C/gas mark 5). Prick the skins of each potato a few times with a fork (to let the moisture escape during cooking).

2 Drizzle a small amount of olive oil on each potato and rub it all over the skin to give it a nice crunchy exterior when cooked. Finally, rub sea salt over the skin.

3 Bake the potatoes directly on the middle rack of the oven for 1¼ to 1¾ hours, or until the skins are very crisp. Toward the end of cooking time, prepare your filling of choice.

4 When ready, remove the potatoes from the oven and cut each in half lengthwise. With a fork, fluff up the potato, then add 1 teaspoon (5 g) Boosted Butter to each half, along with a generous amount of regular butter, and salt and pepper to taste. Mmm.

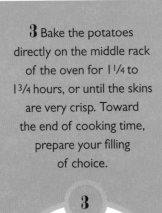

5 Heap some of your chosen topping on each half and serve immediately because, after baked potatoes come out of the oven, they lose their crispness very quickly.

Ganja Garlic Heads

Vampires beware

Of course, not all stoners crave ice cream and cookies when they're high. Some of you like to savor some savories. And few recipes are better than this one, for roasted garlic paste. Of course, garlic breath isn't popular with the opposite sex, so you'll be cuddling fresh air on the couch after scarfing these. But on the flipside, if you've ever suffered paranoid delusions of vampires in your bedroom after a particularly heavy session (we've all been there, brother), rest assured that this will ward the critters off.

I

I Preheat the oven to 375°F (190°C/gas mark 5). Peel away the pale papery outer layers of the garlic bulb skin, leaving the skins of the individual cloves and the bulb itself intact.

How High?:
✳ ✳ ✳

Difficulty:
✳ ✳ ✳

Makin' Time:
15 minutes

Bakin' Time:
30–45 minutes

4 large whole heads of garlic

4 teaspoons (20 ml) Augmented Olive Oil (page 15)

2 tablespoons plus 2 teaspoons olive oil

Sea salt (optional)

Chopped herbs such as thyme or oregano (optional)

Makes 4 heads

NO PAN?
If you don't have a suitable muffin pan, just put the garlic heads in a suitably sized shallow ovenproof dish and wrap them all up in one big foil package.

2 Using a sharp knife, cut ¼ to ½ inch (.5 to 1.25 cm) off the top of the heads, exposing the flesh of each individual clove of the head. Mind those fingers!

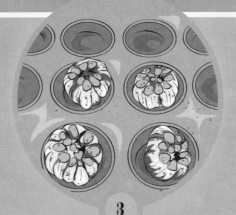

3

2

3 Place the garlic heads in the recesses of a muffin pan. Drizzle a couple of tea-spoons of Augmented Olive Oil over each bulb, using your fingers to make sure the garlic head is well coated. Season the heads with a little salt and sprinkle over some chopped herbs.

4 Cover the pan with foil. Bake in the preheated oven for 30 to 45 minutes, until the garlic cloves feel soft when pressed.

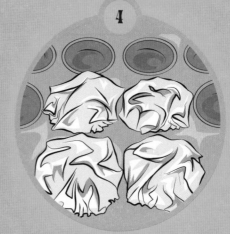

4

5 Allow the garlic to cool sufficiently that you can handle it easily. (Warning: If you've smoked too many reefers today your senses may be dulled.) Using a small knife, cut the skin around the top of each clove. Use your fingers to pull or squeeze the roasted garlic cloves out of their skins.

5

6 Voilà. The finished garlic, ready to apply to your chosen meal (see "Eating Tips").

6

EATING TIPS

These garlic heads are often served as a sweet and creamy accompaniment to roasted and grilled meats and stews. However, there are other options. You can eat the roasted garlic cloves just as they are; mash them with a fork and spread the resulting yummy paste over warm French bread; mix it into sour cream to make a topping for baked potatoes (page 106); or add it to a pasta sauce. If you like things a bit spicy, season the garlic with some cayenne pepper or paprika before covering.

Mighty Marijuana Meatloaf

Hearty high

Long before its name was hijacked by the ample-sized rock-and-roll crooner, meatloaf was a popular dish among hard-working carnivores. Perfect to rebuild strength after a long day toiling in the fields, it's just as delicious if you've spent your day on the less onerous tasks of cooking and smoking out. Don't overdo that Boosted Butter though, or your mind will be racing like a bat out of hell!

How High?:
🍃 🍃 🍃 🍃 🍃

Difficulty:
🍃 🍃 🍃

Makin' Time:
20 minutes

Bakin' Time:
1–1½ hours

I Preheat the oven to 350°F (180°C/gas mark 3) and lightly grease a loaf pan about 9 by 5 by 3 inches (23 by 12.5 by 7.5 cm). In a large mixing bowl, blend the meat and oats together thoroughly.

2 pounds (900 g) lean ground beef

⅔ cup (55 g) rolled oats

1 cup (240 ml) milk

2 tablespoons plus 2 teaspoons (40 g) Boosted Butter (page 12), melted

3 tablespoons plus 1 teaspoon (45 g) butter, melted

2 eggs, well beaten

1 large onion, finely chopped

3 or 4 garlic cloves, finely chopped

2 or 3 celery ribs, finely chopped

2 tablespoons Worcestershire sauce or other good steak sauce

½ cup chopped parsley

1 tablespoon dry mustard

Salt to taste

Freshly ground black pepper to taste

Serves 8

VARIATIONS

For an interesting change in flavor, try beef broth or tomato juice in place of milk, or spread the top of the loaf with chile sauce or ketchup just before putting it in the oven. To make the meatloaf into a meal in itself, add some frozen peas or mixed vegetables to the mixture.

3

4 Transfer to the prepared loaf pan and bake uncovered for 1 to 1½ hours, until nicely browned on top and a toothpick inserted into the center comes out dry.

3 Add this to the meat mixture. Add the remaining ingredients and stir until thoroughly blended.

4

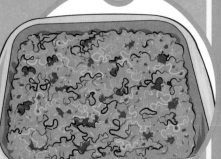

2 In a small bowl, combine the milk, melted butters, and eggs.

2

5

5 Baste (see box) with any juices around the edges. Return to the oven for 5 minutes.

6 Remove from the oven. Let the loaf stand in the pan a few minutes before turning it out on a warmed serving platter. Cut into thick slices to serve.

6

KITCHEN TERM

Baste means to pour juices or melted fat over meat during cooking in order to keep it moist.

Pigs in Blankets

Winter warmers

Admittedly, this dish does not have the most appetizing of names, but these pigs in blankets smell delicious while cooking in the oven, and they taste even better. They're great for winter holidays—when you've polished off a couple of these, snuggle up in your own blanket and prepare to snooze the day away.

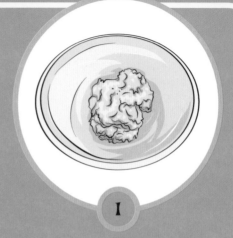

I

How High?:
🌿🌿🌿🌿

Difficulty:
🌿🌿🌿🌿🌿

Makin' Time:
30 minutes, plus
30 minutes chillin'

Bakin' Time:
35–45 minutes

3 ½ cups [400 g] all-purpose flour, plus additional for rolling

½ teaspoon salt

3 tablespoons [40 g] Boosted Butter [page 12], chilled

¼ cup plus 1 tablespoon [75 g] butter, chilled

About ⅔ cup [150 ml] ice cold water

1 pound [450 g] raw lean sausage meat, removed from casings

1 egg yolk

2 tablespoons milk

Makes about 8 pigs

I Sift the flour and salt into a bowl. Place the two butters in a separate bowl and gently toss. Cut in two-thirds of the butter mixture, until the flour resembles breadcrumbs. Carefully cut in the remaining butter, taking care to leave it in small pieces. Stir in just enough of the cold water, a little at a time, for a dough to form. Chill for at least 30 minutes. Time for a reefer, methinks.

2 Preheat the oven to 350°F (180°C/gas mark 4). On a floured surface, roll the pastry out into a rectangle about 12 by 6 inches (30 by 15 cm). Cut this crosswise to make 2 strips about 6 inches (15 cm) across.

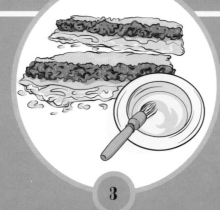

3

4 Cut each log crosswise into 3-inch (8-cm) lengths.

2

3 Divide the sausage into 2 equal portions. Position the sausage meat in a long continuous roll along the middle of each piece of dough. Make an egg wash by lightly beating the egg yolk and then beating in the milk in a small bowl. Brush one edge of one of the pieces of pastry with egg wash (to help seal the pastry), parallel with the sausage meat, and roll the pastry over to form a long sausage roll. Repeat with the other piece of dough.

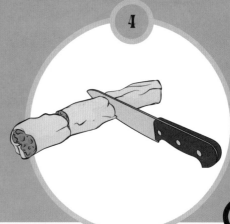

4

SALIVATIN' SAVORY BAKES

5 Position on the wire rack over a foil-lined baking sheet (to catch the dripping fat during baking). Using a sharp knife (be careful), cut slits in the tops of the rolls, and then brush all over with the egg wash.

6 Bake for 35 to 45 minutes, until the pastry is golden brown and the sausage meat is cooked through.

7 Let the rolls cool; otherwise they'll take the skin off the roof of your mouth. Enjoy.

VEGGIE OPTION

Those who don't eat meat can make this recipe using wheat meat or other meat substitute.

Herbal Quiche

A savory session

You can enjoy this perfect picnic food surreptitiously at an outdoor family gathering, or gorge on it with your buddies, stoned out of your mind, at a music festival. You decide. However you eat it, this recipe is a real blast.

I To make the pastry, in a food processor pulse the flour with the salt. Add the butters and pulse about 10 times until the butter pieces are the size of small peas. You can also do this by hand in a bowl with a pastry blender or knife.

How High?:

🍁 🍁 🍁 🍁 🍁

Difficulty:

🍁 🍁 🍁 🍁

Makin' Time:

30 minutes, plus 30 minutes chillin'

Bakin' Time:

About 1 1/4 hours

Pastry

1 1/4 cups (150 g) all-purpose flour, plus additional for rolling

1/4 teaspoon salt

3 tablespoons (45 g) Boosted Butter (page 12), chilled and cubed

3 tablespoons (45 g) butter, chilled and cubed

1 egg yolk

Filling

1 onion, finely chopped

1 tablespoon olive oil

2 large eggs

1 large egg yolk

1 1/4 cups (300 ml) heavy cream

Salt to taste

Freshly ground black pepper to taste

1 teaspoon chopped thyme leaves

2 tablespoons chopped flat-leaf parsley

Handful of basil leaves, torn

4 ounces (115 g) brie cheese, diced

Makes 1 10-inch (25-cm) pie

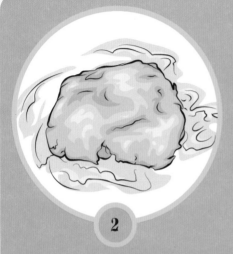

2

2 Add the egg yolk and 2 tablespoons cold water, and pulse until the pastry starts to come together. Turn out onto a floured work surface and knead 2 or 3 times, just until smooth. Pat the pastry into a round, wrap in plastic wrap, and chill until firm, about 20 minutes.

3 Preheat the oven to 375°F (190°C/gas mark 5). On a floured surface, roll the pastry out to a 12-inch (30-cm) round. Now for the tricky part. Ease this into a 10-inch (25-cm) fluted tart pan with a removable bottom, without stretching it. Trim away any excess pastry with a knife (use the extra to patch any holes) and chill the tart shell for 10 minutes.

3

BLIND BAKING
Using the foil and beans is a neat trick to stop the inner base from rising as it bakes. In the culinary world it's called "blind baking."

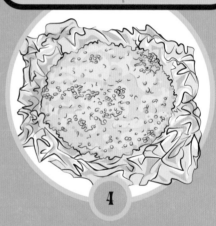

4

4 Line the tart shell with foil and fill with dried beans. Bake for 30 minutes, just until dry.

5 While the shell is in the oven, make the filling. In a large skillet, sauté the onion in the olive oil over moderate heat (don't rub your eyes!), stirring, until softened, about 5 minutes. Transfer to a bowl and let cool.

6

5

6 In a bowl, whisk together the eggs with the egg yolk and cream. Season with salt and pepper. Stir in the herbs.

7 Remove the beans and foil and put the tart shell back in the oven for about 10 minutes more, until golden. Transfer the tart pan to a sturdy baking sheet.

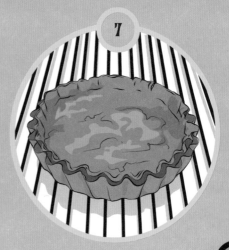

7

8 Scatter the cooled onion and the cheese over the base of the pastry shell and then carefully pour the egg and herb mixture over. Mmm, this is looking good.

9 Bake for 25 to 30 minutes, until the topping is just firm but still wobbles slightly if the pan is moved. Rotate the sheet halfway through for even baking, and remove when the quiche is puffed up and lightly browned.

10 Transfer to a rack and let cool for 15 minutes. Remove the ring, cut the quiche into wedges and serve either warm or cold.

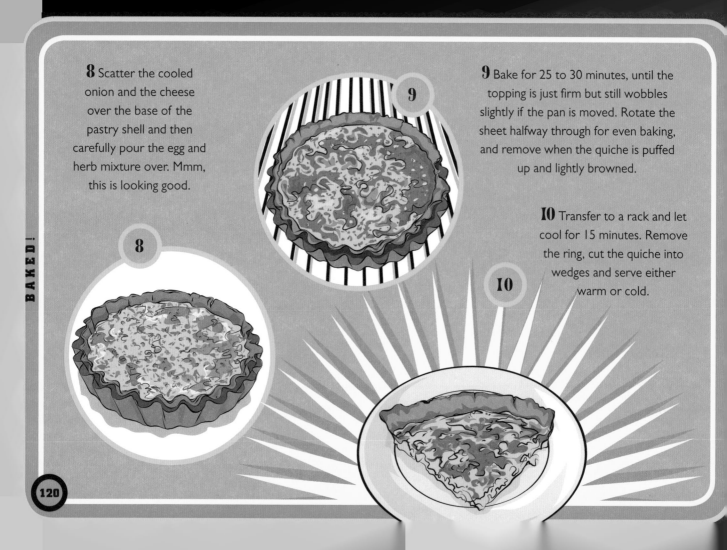

Pot Pizza

Big slice of fun

If your idea of a perfect night in with your buddies is a few beers, a few more smokes, and a pizza, then this recipe, with the magic ingredient of Augmented Olive Oil, is just the thing. A staple of the Mediterranean diet, olive oil has never tasted so good—although it won't lubricate your brain much. Duh!

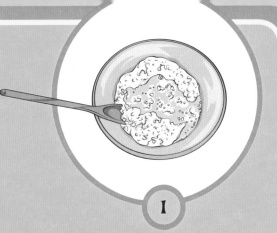

I

How High?:
🍁 🍁 🍁 🍁

Difficulty:
🍁 🍁 🍁 🍁

Makin' Time:
30 minutes, plus about 1 1/2 hours restin', chillin', and risin'

Bakin' Time:
About 30 minutes

Pizza dough

4 1/2 cups (675 g) bread flour, plus additional for rolling

1/4-ounce (7-g) package of quick-rising active dry yeast

Pinch of salt

2 tablespoons olive oil

2 tablespoons plus 2 teaspoons (40 ml) Augmented Olive Oil (page 15)

For the topping

2 tablespoons olive oil

2 large red onions, halved and sliced

Handful of rosemary sprigs

About 12 cherry tomatoes, halved

Sea salt

Serves 8

I To make the dough, combine the flour, yeast, and salt in a large bowl. Make a well in the middle, pour in both the oils and about I cup of lukewarm water. Using a wooden spoon, mix the flour, Augmented Olive Oil, and water together until they become a slightly wet dough, adding a little more water if necessary.

2 Tip the dough out onto a lightly floured surface and knead for at least 10 minutes until smooth and elastic.

3 Place the dough in an oiled bowl, cover with plastic wrap, and leave to rise in a warm place until doubled in size, about 1 hour.

4 When the dough has risen, gently punch it down and stretch it to fit a small rimmed baking sheet about 10 by 13 inches (25 by 35 cm). Leave to rise for about 20 minutes.

PROVE YOURSELF

Proofing means aerating dough—that is, rising, or getting bigger before your eyes. This is one of the many magic elements of cooking. Amaze your disbelieving stoner pals. Awesome!

5 While the dough is proofing, place the onions and 1 tablespoon olive oil in a skillet and sauté until soft, about 5 minutes. Set aside.

5

6 Preheat the oven to 400°F (200°C/gas mark 6). Spread the cooked onions over the dough and scatter with the rosemary. Use your finger to make little dimples all over the dough, drizzle the remaining oil over, put the tomato halves sliced side down in the dimples, and lightly sprinkle the salt over the top.

6

7

7 Bake for about 30 minutes until the crust is golden. Let cool slightly, cut into squares, and serve.

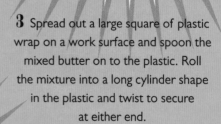

Shakin' Sides

If you want to jazz up any of your existing recipes (or simply want to increase your intake of chronic) try these side dishes.

Bashin' Butter

Use this lovely herbed butter on top of grilled steaks, fish, or vegetables. If you want to give it a bit more bite, add a couple of peeled and crushed garlic cloves to the mixture.

1 cup (225 g) Boosted Butter
(page 12), at room
temperature

1/4 cup chopped flat-leaf
parsley leaves

3 tablespoons lemon juice

Makes about 1 cup

I In a large bowl, mash the butter with a fork.

2 Add the parsley and lemon juice, and continue mashing and mixing until the ingredients are all well blended.

3 Spread out a large square of plastic wrap on a work surface and spoon the mixed butter on to the plastic. Roll the mixture into a long cylinder shape in the plastic and twist to secure at either end.

4 Chill or freeze until needed. To use, cut thick slices from the butter roll and put one on each steak, piece of fish, or other food item as you serve it.

Chargin' Cream Sauce

This is really a basic white sauce made with cream, but it can be very easily adapted into all sorts of other sauces for lots of uses.

1/4 cup (55 g) Boosted Butter (page 12)

4 tablespoons (37 g) all-purpose flour

2 cups milk or cream, or equal parts of each

Salt

White pepper

Makes about 2 1/2 cups

REFINING YOUR SAUCE

For a béchamel sauce for things like moussaka, add some bay leaves and cooked chopped onion.

For a cheese sauce, add some freshly grated nutmeg, a little mustard, and grated cheese of your choice to taste. Add 1/3 cup of grated Parmesan cheese for an Alfredo pasta sauce.

1 In a large, heavy saucepan over low heat melt the Boosted Butter. Add the flour and cook, stirring constantly, just until the flour and butter are well incorporated. (If you want a sauce with a nutty flavor, then cook the flour and butter a bit longer until it colors slightly.)

2 Gradually add the milk or cream, stirring constantly, until the mixture thickens and comes to a boil. Simmer very gently for a minute or two to cook out the floury taste.

3 Season to taste with salt and white pepper.

Shotgun Salsa

This spicy salsa dip couldn't be easier to make, although it does contain a huge array of ingredients, and really packs a punch.

6 ripe tomatoes, diced

1 small red onion, diced small

1 or 2 chile peppers, diced small [seeds and membrane removed if you prefer]

1/2 teaspoon freshly ground black pepper

1/2 teaspoon salt

2 garlic cloves, finely minced

1/4 cup [60 ml] Augmented Olive Oil [page 15]

1/4 cup [60 ml] lime juice

2 or 3 teaspoons chopped fresh cilantro leaves

Pinch of dried oregano

Pinch of ground cumin

Makes about 3 cups

1 In a large bowl, combine all ingredients and leave for at least an hour to let the flavors get friendly.

2 Serve as a dip with tortilla chips or as an accompaniment to burgers, broiled or grilled chicken, or pork chops.

Jive Jam

This is not so much a recipe as a suggestion. Simply stir some ground cannabis into a new jar of your favorite jelly, jam, or marmalade, reseal and leave for a day or two to let the good stuff permeate the contents of the jar, then use whenever you need a sweet lift. Check our suggested dosage quantities on page 17 for the amount to add, remembering to adjust for how thick you like to lay it on. You can do the same with jarred peanut butter.

SAVORY SOLUTION

You needn't restrict yourself to giving sweet preserves this treatment, you can do the same with bottled sauces (even tomato ketchup), salsas, pickles, relishes, mustards, chutneys, and so on.

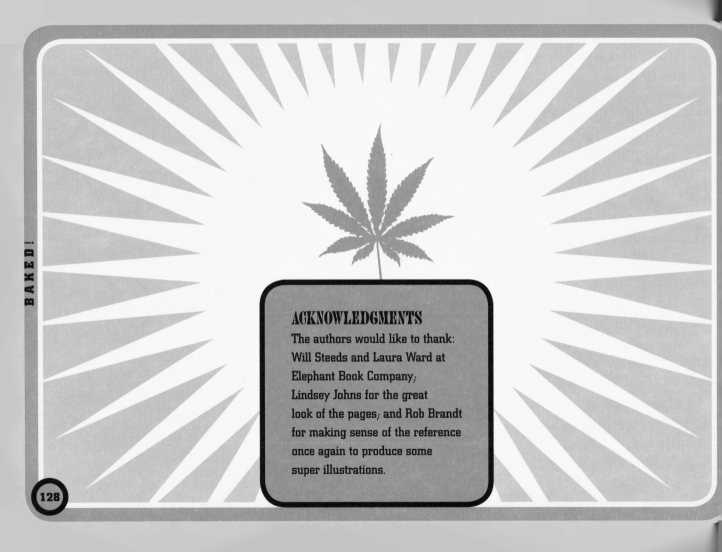

ACKNOWLEDGMENTS

The authors would like to thank:
Will Steeds and Laura Ward at
Elephant Book Company;
Lindsey Johns for the great
look of the pages; and Rob Brandt
for making sense of the reference
once again to produce some
super illustrations.